Nye

T0024421

Tim Price

methuen | drama

LONDON • NEW YORK • OXFORD • NEW DELHI • SYDNEY

METHUEN DRAMA
Bloomsbury Publishing Plc
50 Bedford Square, London, WC1B 3DP, UK
1385 Broadway, New York, NY 10018, USA
29 Earlsfort Terrace, Dublin 2, Ireland

BLOOMSBURY, METHUEN DRAMA and the Methuen
Drama logo are trademarks of Bloomsbury Publishing Plc

First published in Great Britain 2024

Photography (Michael Sheen) by Rachel Louise Brown

Art direction and design by National Theatre Graphic Design Studio

A catalogue record for this book is available from the British Library.

A catalog record for this book is available from the Library of Congress.

ISBN: PB: 978-1-3504-7197-9
ePDF: 978-1-3504-7198-6
eBook: 978-1-3504-7199-3

Series: Modern Plays

Typeset by Mark Heslington Ltd, Scarborough, North Yorkshire

To find out more about our authors and books visit
www.bloomsbury.com and sign up for our newsletters.

Nye

A new play by Tim Price
A co-production with Wales Millennium Centre

Cast, *in alphabetical order*

Gwen Davies	**Remy Beasley**
Mr Orchard/Mr Francis	**Matthew Bulgo**
Speaker/Luke Williams/Councillor Williams	**Dyfan Dwyfor**
Archie Lush	**Roger Evans**
Clerk/Ross Doherty	**Ross Foley**
Herbert Morrison MP/Mr Howells	**Jon Furlong**
Neil Jones	**Daniel Hawksford**
Mrs Jones/Cleaner	**Bea Holland**
Clement Attlee/Matron	**Stephanie Jacob**
Nurse Ellie/Arianwen	**Kezrena James**
Doctor Dain/Winston Churchill	**Tony Jayawardena**
Owen Thomas/Councillor Morgan	**Michael Keane**
Neville Chamberlain//Dr Frankel/Mr Hill/Doctor Voiceover	**Nicholas Khan**
Lucy Pritchard/Doctor Voiceover	**Rebecca Killick**
Ensemble	**Oliver Llewellyn-Jenkins**
Mark Smith/Mr Leslie/Graham the Porter	**Mark Matthews**
David Bevan/Councillor Hopkins/Doctor Voiceover	**Rhodri Meilir**
William Jones/Mr Llywellyn/Chris the Porter	**Ashley Mejri**
Jack Stockton	**Lee Mengo**
Mr Fury	**David Monteith**
Ensemble	**Mali O'Donnell**
Sara Roberts/Mrs Lewis	**Sara Otung**
Aneurin 'Nye' Bevan	**Michael Sheen**
Jennie Lee	**Sharon Small**

Understudies

Mr Orchard/Neville Chamberlain/David Bevan/Dr Frankel	**Ross Foley**
Archie Lush	**Dyfan Dwyfor**
Herbert Morrison MP	**Michael Keane**

Clement Attlee/Jennie Lee	**Bea Holland**
Nurse Ellie/Arianwen	**Sara Otung**
Doctor Dain/Winston Churchill	**David Monteith**
Aneurin 'Nye' Bevan	**Lee Mengo**

All other roles played by members of the company.

Swings	**Oliver Llewellyn-Jenkins and Mali O'Donnell**

Big band and brass band music recorded at Air Lyndhurst and engineered by Jeremy Murphy.

Trumpet and Cornet	**Ryan Quigley**
Trumpet and Cornet	**Simon Gardner**
Trumpet dbl and Soprano Cornet	**Rebecca Crawshaw**
Trumpet and Cornet	**Chris Snead**
Trombone 1	**Andy Wood**
Trombone 2 dbl Euphonium	**Barnaby Philpott**
Trombone 3 dbl Euphonium	**Jane Salmon**
Bass Trombone dbl Tuba	**Barry Clements**
Alto Saxophone	**Howard McGill**
Alto Saxophone	**Jennie Chilton**
Tenor Saxophone	**Nick Moss**
Tenor Saxophone	**Jessamy Holder**
Baritone Saxophone	**Claire McInerney**
Double Bass	**Laurence Ungless**
Drumkit	**Tom Clare**
Piano	**Clive Dunstall**
Guitar	**Justin Quinn**

Additional music recorded at Air Edel and engineered by Nick Taylor.

Violin	**John Mills**
Violin	**Jeremy Isaac**
Viola	**Lydia Northcott**
Cello	**Bozidar Vukotic**
Cello	**Vicky Matthews**
Bass	**Laurence Ungless**
Director	**Rufus Norris**
Set Designer	**Vicki Mortimer**
Costume Designer	**Kinnetia Isidore**
Lighting Designer	**Paule Constable**

Co-Choreographers	**Steven Hoggett and Jess Williams**
Composer	**Will Stuart**
Sound Designer	**Donato Wharton**
Projection Designer	**Jon Driscoll**
Casting	**Alastair Coomer CDG and Chloe Blake**
Dialect Coach	**Patricia Logue**
Company Voice Work	**Cathleen McCarron and Tamsin Newlands**
Consultant Medical Adviser	**Matt Morgan**
Associate Director	**Francesca Goodridge**
Associate Set Designer	**Matt Hellyer**
Associate Costume Designer	**Zoë Thomas-Webb**
Producer	**Pádraig Cusack**
Production Manager	**Jim Leaver**
Dramaturg	**Stewart Pringle**
Company Stage Manager	**Shane Thom**
Deputy Stage Manager	**Anna Hill**
Assistant Stage Managers	**Sophie Mclean and Jo Phipps**
Deputy Production Manager	**Tabitha Piggott**
Production Assistant	**TJ Nash**
Movement Captain	**Rebecca Killick**
Project Draughting	**Alan Bain**
Digital Art	**Daniel Radley-Bennett**
Costume Supervisor	**Zoë Thomas-Webb**
Assistant Costume Supervisor	**Sydney Florence**
Wigs, Hair and Make-up Supervisor	**Kim Kasim**
Running Wardrobe Supervisor	**Ruth Williams**
Props Supervisor	**Chris Lake**
Props Buyer	**Laura Flowers**
Props Making Manager	**Michael Garrett**
Props Making Coordinator	**Michelle McLucas**
Lighting Supervisor	**Sam McLeod**
Lighting Programmer	**Will Frost**
Production Sound Engineer	**James Wickens**
Sound Operator	**Nick Mann**
Radio Mics Supervisor	**Indi Brodley**
Radio Mics Technician	**Marie Zschlommler**

Sound Technicians	**Claire Stamp and Jason Yu**
Film Lighting Gaffer	**Huw Llewellyn**
Projection Design Associate	**Gemma Carrington**
Production Video Engineer	**George Jarvis**
Video Programmer	**Dylan Marsh**
Video System Engineer	**Adrien Corcilius**
Video Technician	**Jason Hyde**
Stage Supervisor	**Dave Tuff**
Automation	**Phil Horsburgh**
Rigging Supervisor	**Duncan Weir**
Construction Supervisor	**Paul Sheppard**
Scenic Art Supervisor	**Alice Collie**
Production Photographer	**Johan Persson**

Nye was first performed at the Olivier Theatre, London, on 6 March 2024, before transferring to Wales Millennium Centre, Cardiff, from 18 May to 1 June 2024.

Thanks

Rufus Norris, Kate Varah and all at the National Theatre. Ben Power, Sarah Clarke, Sarah Corke, Nina Steiger, Stewart Pringle and all at the NT Studio. Graeme Farrow and all at the Wales Millennium Centre, Pádraig Cusack, Michael Sheen, Roger Evans, Remy Beasley, Sharon Small, Lee Mengo, Dan Hawksford, Matt Bulgo, Francesca Goodridge, Jess Williams, Steven Hogget, Paule Constable, Vicki Mortimer, Will Stuart, Donato Wharton, Kinnetia Isidore, Patricia Logue, Meredydd Barker, Hamish Pirie, Mawgaine Tarrant-Cornish, Dr Matt Morgan, Dr Lara McMillan, The King of the North, Cathy King and all at 42, Big Pit, Neil Kinnock, The South Wales Miners' Museum, Councillor Alyson Tippings and all at Tredegar Town Council, Phil, Menna, Matthew, Maryline, Joseph and Sophia Price, Franklin Moss Price, Martha Moss Price, Chloë Moss, Gary Marsh, Mark Jefferies.

Author's Note

This play took over ten years to write, and I was lucky enough to make it with actors who I have worked with for over twenty years. It is a great comfort to look at the cast list and see decades-long friendships. During the writing of this play we lost a friend, one of the finest actors Wales has produced. While he had nothing to do with the show, if he was still with us there is no doubt he would have been in the room and on the stage beside us. His name isn't in the cast list but it feels right that his name is in this book because whatever we do, he is still very much with us and always will be – Alex Beckett.

Nye

For Fizzy Oppe

Our mother tree in our forest of friendship

With love here and hereafter

Always and forever

Tim x

Cast

Nye Bevan, *various ages, Welsh*
Jennie Lee, *various ages, Scottish*
Nurse Ellie/Arianwen, *twenties*
Dr Dain/Winston Churchill, *forties/eighties*
David Bevan, *various ages, Welsh*
Neville Chamberlain/Dr Frankel, *forties, English*
Archie Lush, *various ages, Welsh*
Clement Attlee/Matron, *fifties, English*
Patient 1/Herbert Morrison MP, *fifties, English*
Lucy Prichard, *nine and twenty-one, Welsh*
Alun Jones, *nine, Welsh*
Owen Thomas, *nine, Welsh*
Luke Williams, *nine, Welsh*
Mark Smith, *nine, Welsh*
Sarah Roberts, *nine, Welsh*
William Jones, *nine, Welsh*
Ross Doherty, *nine, Welsh*

Jack Stockton, *twenty-one, Welsh*
Gwen Davies, *twenty-one, Welsh*
Neil Jones, *twenty-one, Welsh*
Councillor Jones, *Tredegar Iron and Coal Company (any)*
Councillor Hopkins, *Tredegar Iron and Coal Company (any)*
Councillor Williams, *Tredegar Iron and Coal Company (any)*
Clerk, *any*
Tory MPs 1–5
Patients 1–22
The Cleaner
Graham the Porter
Chris the Porter
Speaker
Mr Howells
Mrs Jones
Mr Hill
Mr Llywelyn
Mr Fury
Mrs Lewis

Doctor Voiceover

Death

Author's note

/ indicates when the next line should start being spoken.

. . . indicates the trailing off of a thought.

– indicates an interruption of thought.

() means a word that Nye was trying to say but gives up and switches to another.

Bold *words mean the word could be treated by sound design.*

On stuttering

Like all stutters, Nye's changed and evolved throughout his life; as he gained more control with age, new sounds became more difficult. The text suggests where stuttering is likely to have occurred and when, but it is also for the performer to find where these might occur. Plosive sounds, alevolar consonants, the voiceless alevolar sibilant at the start of words.

Prologue

NHS Royal Free Hospital Hampstead 1960

Fantasia – sound design swell.

In his pyjamas, **Nye** *stands.*

Death*'s hands engulf* **Nye.**

Nye *screams, terrified.*

Nye   ARIANWEEEEN! HELP!

Lights down.

Scene One

NHS Royal Free Hospital Hampstead 1960

A busy NHS ward. Doctors and nurses attend to various patients.

Upstage sits **Matron** *at a desk with a lamp.*

Archie *and* **Jennie** *pace back and forth.*

Matron   Patient incoming.

Being pushed by a porter – **Nye** *is wheeled onto the ward.*

His arrival is noted by patients and nurses – a pause as he is taken to his bay.

As **Nye** *is settled into his bay:*

A patient nearby behind curtains struggles to breathe and wheezes in an oxygen mask.

A patient struggles to walk with a cane.

Another patient sits reading a newspaper.

A manual buzzer sounds as patients call for a nurse.

On the radio somewhere, 'Get Happy' plays.

Archie   OK. (*Discreet.*) Are you OK?

Jennie (*discreet*)   I'm OK.

Archie *gives* **Jennie** *an awkward hug.*

Archie (*discreet*)   Gonna be OK. We'll do it together.

Nye *is grimacing.*

Nye   Hmmmaaw . . .

Jennie   He's coming round. He's coming round.

Nye   Hmammma . . .

Nye *shifts uncomfortably.*

Archie   He's waking up. He's waking up . . .

Archie   Here he is. Hello.

Jennie   Nye?

Nye   Jennie.

Jennie   Here I am. I'm here.

Nye *puts his arms out to her, they hug. He kisses her.*

Nye   Archie?

Archie   Alright butt?

Nye *puts an arm out for* **Archie**.

Jennie   How are you feeling?

Nye   Awful.

Nye *is grimacing.*

Jennie   Try and lie still, you've just had an operation.

Nye *shifts again wincing.*

Nye   Where am I?

Jennie   The recovery ward.

Archie   You had an operation. The ulcer?

Jennie   You're in hospital.

Archie   Remember?

Jennie   The nurses have been *wonderful*. They've been coming to check on you. Making sure everything's OK.

Nye   It hurts.

Jennie   You've had an operation. You're in a hospital.

Archie   Hospital you built. Look.

This lands with **Nye**.

He blinks.

Nye   Look.

Slowly, he becomes more conscious of his surroundings, he sits up, and takes in the surrounding ward.

He sees socialised medicine in action:

1) A patient passing in a wheelchair.

2) A nurse putting flowers into a vase for a patient.

3) A librarian pushing a trolley of books.

4) A patient wearing an oxygen mask, doctors listening to his chest.

5) Nurses helping a patient learn to walk with a with a crutch.

6) A curtain animating as a nurse finds her way out.

Nye *turns to* **Jennie** *with the biggest broadest smile –* **Jennie** *has to hide her heart breaking.*

Archie   I'll, uh. I'll see if the doctor is free.

Nye   So nice. Seeing it. Without everyone . . . standing on ceremony. Isn't it?

Beat.

Look at what we did.

Jennie   Nye, / there's something . . .

Nye   And there's more to do.

Jennie   Darling . . .

Nye   I'm fine. I'm not going anywhere. Except maybe Number 10.

Dr Dain *appears.*

Dr Dain   Mr Bevan. Good to see you're awake. How are you feeling?

Nye   Bit rough.

Dr Dain   It'll take some time for the effects of the anaesthetic to wear off. Are you comfortable? Would you like me to come back later?

Jennie   Yes, maybe later.

Nye   No no, it's fine. Go ahead.

Dr Dain   Are you sure?

Nye   Yes yes.

Dr Dain   OK. Mind if I examine you?

Nye   Go ahead.

Dr Dain   Deep breath for me. One more, good.

Dr Dain *checks* **Nye***'s pulse. He shines a torch in* **Nye***'s eye. He examines* **Nye***'s surgical wound.*

Dr Dain   All looking as it should. Mr Bevan, I need to talk you through some things with the operation. It was meant to be a two-hour procedure, but in the end, we kept you under for six hours continuous.

Nye   Why so long? You got the ulcer, didn't you?

Dr Dain   So.

Jennie   Yes! Yes, they got it. All went fine.

A moment between **Jennie** *and* **Dr Dain***.*

Jennie   It was fine. Wasn't it? You just need to be careful. And get plenty of rest. Doctor, you can you tell him, can't you? Everything went fine. Didn't it?

Jennie *is imploring.*

Dr Dain   Yes. I performed a, a laparotomy. And I found a large, duodenal, ulcer. About an inch and a quarter by an inch. Then we used an omentum patch, some fatty tissue, to patch over the top. There were no complications, beyond finding such a big ulcer, which is why it took so long. So, bed rest for three weeks.

Nye   When can I leave?

Dr Dain   Let's focus on getting better, shall we?

Nye   I want to get back to work.

Nye *grimaces in pain.*

Jennie   You'll be back to work soon. Won't he, Doctor?

Beat.

Dr Dain   I can't see why you can't be back at work. Soon. We tell people, no lifting for at least three months.

Nye   Can I – AAAHhh . . .

Nye *writhes in pain.*

Jennie   What is it? Doctor! What's wrong?

Dr Dain   Try not to move too much, Mr Bevan . . . it will subside.

Jennie   What's happening, Doctor?

Dr Dain *presses a buzzer – 'Buzzer!'*

Matron *approaches.*

Dr Dain   Matron, a fifth of a grain of morphine please.

Matron *leaves.*

Nye   HELP! AAhhhh

Jennie   What is going on? Is this . . . the operation or . . .

Dr Dain   Mr Bevan, deep breaths if you can . . .

Nye *writhes in pain before eventually collapsing back in his bed exhausted.*

Dr Dain   Can we move Mr Bevan to bay seven?

Porters appear and start to move **Nye**. **Dr Dain** *walks with him.*

Jennie   Where are you taking him?

Dr Dain   Just somewhere with a little more privacy.

Nye   AHH, JESUS CHRIST!

Nye *tries to grab something.*

Matron   Mr Dain, some pentobarbital maybe?

Dr Dain   Yes. Two grains please.

Matron   This will make things more comfortable, Mr Bevan.

Nurse Ellie *fits the drip to* **Nye**'s *hand.*

Jennie   He's in a lot of pain.

Nye   Please can you do something?

Nurse Ellie   This will take care of it, Mr Bevan, just a few minutes and you'll start to feel the difference.

Jennie   Is this . . . uh, *normal?*

Matron *helps* **Nurse Ellie** *with the drugs.*

Dr Dain   Could I speak to you outside?

Jennie   Uh. Yes. Yes of course.

Jennie *stands up, she doesn't want to leave* **Nye**.

She kisses **Nye** *and eventually follows* **Dr Dain** *out.*

Nye   Can I have a drink?

Nurse Ellie   Some water?

Nye   A drink drink.

Beat.

Whiskey.

Nurse Ellie   You can't get whiskey on the NHS, Mr Bevan.

Nye   Well, that's a bloody oversight.

Nurse Ellie   This shouldn't take too long before you start to feel more comfortable.

Nye *groans.*

Nye   Talk to me. Distract me.

Nurse Ellie   I can't tell you the number of girls I've had offering to swap shifts with me.

Nye   What for?

Nurse Ellie   Everyone wants to look after you.

Nye   Does everyone know I'm here?

Nurse Ellie   Well. Not officially, no. But, we're *nurses.*

Nye   Oh God. Everyone knows. Be in the bloody *Daily Mail* tomorrow.

Nurse Ellie   No, they just want to know what you're like. One girl wanted to know what you're reading? What colour your pyjamas are?

The pain begins to subside.

Nye   I hope you said I'm the best dressed patient you've ever had.

Nurse Ellie   Absolutely, I can't lie about that. Feeling anything now?

Nye   Hmm . . . not sure. Still a bit . . .

Nurse Ellie   Can you try counting back from ten for me?

Nye   Ten . . . Nine . . .

Nurse Ellie   That's right . . .

Nye   Eight . . .

Nurse Ellie   It's funny being this close to you.

Nye   Seven . . .

Nurse Ellie   I went to see you speak once.

Nye   Six . . .

Nurse Ellie   My sister and I came down from Nottingham. Keep counting . . .

Nye   Five . . .

Nurse Ellie   I was already signed up for nursing, and she was doing a secretarial course . . .

Nye   Four.

Nurse Ellie   But after seeing you speak she switched to nursing like me.

Nye   Three

Nurse Ellie   She's at Bart's now. We could barely see you and now look, I'm tucking you in.

Nye   Two . . .

Nurse Ellie   Making sure you're comfortable. I'm going to look after you, I promise. And then, I'm gonna tell my sister.

Scene Two

Family home 1925

Nye   Sister.

Arianwen   You're late.

Nye *turns and he sees his sister* **Arianwen** *who is also, somehow,* **Nurse Ellie**.

Nye   I'm uh . . .

Arianwen   You're late, Nye.

Nye   I was just . . .

Arianwen   How come you're so late? What happened?

Nye   I dunno. Archie was there.

Arianwen   Going over the cases for tomorrow.

Nye   Yeah, I think so.

Arianwen   Did they give you a room in the club?

Nye   I can't remember.

Arianwen   Have you eaten?

Nye *feels his stomach, it's sore.*

Nye   Um . . . I'll be OK.

Arianwen   You need to eat, there's soup.

Nye   It's fine.

Arianwen *hands him some soup.*

Nye   I'm fine.

Arianwen   No, you need to eat, you probably haven't eaten all day. You can't be a miner's agent if you're fainting at tribunals.

Eventually **Nye** *concedes and eats the soup.*

Arianwen   How did you get home?

Nye   Wwww-walked.

Arianwen   Why didn't you get the bus?

Nye   I fancied a ww-walk.

Arianwen   With all your papers?

Nye   I fancied the walk.

Arianwen   Up the hill with your papers? Were the buses running?

Nye   Yeah mh-but it's ff-fine.

Arianwen *goes to a purse and puts a coin on his soup tray.*

Nye *stares at it.*

Arianwen   Mrs Richards Garw Nant, paid for her curtains in advance.

Nye   I don't mind walking.

Arianwen   I don't want you coming home exhausted and falling asleep in the chair.

Arianwen *pushes the coin towards him.*

Nye *takes it.*

Nye   I'll pay you bbmh-back. That was d-d (delicious) tasty, thank you.

Nye *gets up to leave.*

Arianwen   Get the bus tomorrow.

Nye   Yeah, I'll try.

Arianwen   No.

Beat.

Get the bus. Get home a bit earlier.

Nye   I've got a lot on / with all the cases.

Arianwen   I know.

Nye   I've got three hearings / this w-week.

Arianwen   I'm not saying you're not busy. Just get home a bit earlier.

Nye   If I can't get men bbmh-back into w-work then they're destitute / Arianwen.

Arianwen   I know.

Nye   I've got whole fff-families relying on me.

Arianwen   So this family can't rely on you?

Nye   What do you ww-want from me? You've been on pins since I got in.

Arianwen   I want you to come home on time.

Nye   Fine. I'll come home on time.

Arianwen   And then when you come home on time, I want you to sit with Dad, someone needs to sit with him all the time now and if you start doing your bit then it means Mam and I can have a rest.

Nye   Do you have any *idea* how much reading I've got to do?

Arianwen   Do you have any idea what I've got on? I've got my sewing work. I'm caring for Dad. / I'm doing housework for Mam. I'm getting medicines. Shopping. Cooking your tea. And it seems all you do, is your Union work which doesn't pay enough even for a bus fare.

Nye   OK OK.

Arianwen   I'm sorry. But. It's Dad! You've always put him on a pedestal. Why don't you care?

Nye   I do cc-care.

Arianwen   Then show it.

Nye   You're better at looking after him than me.

Arianwen   I'm better than you at everything. / Doesn't mean I should do everything.

Nye   Right, I'm done here.

Nye *turns and leaves.*

Arianwen He asked after you.

Nye *stops in his tracks . . .*

Nye What, what did he say?

Arianwen 'Where's Nye?'

Nye That's all?

Arianwen Well, that nearly killed him. And if he has to ask again, it might kill him.

Nye That's all he said?

Arianwen That's all he could say.

Nye Has the doctor been?

Arianwen He's been.

Nye What did he ss-say?

Arianwen What he always says, steam and tonic, steam and tonic. Up and down the valley.

Nye That's why we need to try and a-get compensation / we need to

Arianwen Dad doesn't want compensation.

Nye He bloody should, we need to / take the case to the

Arianwen Dad doesn't want money.

Nye It's not about the money, it's about natural justice, it's about somebody seeing / what he's going through.

Arianwen Dad doesn't want anyone to see what he's going through, / he wants privacy and his family.

Nye No-one's looking at our lives and thinking it's not fair that men are dying in their fifties. Or that children have got rickets. Or that women are dying of childbed fever. No-one's thinking about us. So we have to mhp-p (push) fight for every grain of justice or fairness. And this is not fair. And if no-one will speak for us then I will.

Arianwen   The thing that you're not hearing is, no-one is asking you to.

Pause.

Nye   Mh mh-but . . . I cc-can. I can get justice

Arianwen   No-one is asking you to do this though, Nye.

Nye   I can fix things / I can mh-p-p (put) make things right.

Arianwen   No-one wants you to fix things. No-one expects you to fix things. Dad doesn't want you to fix things. He just wants to see you before he dies.

Arianwen *leaves . . .*

Nye *turns to his father's bed.*

Filled with fear, he pulls a curtain . . .

Scene Three

Sirhowy Elementary School 1908

*To reveal his childhood classmates (**Neil Jones**, **Gwen Davies**, **Owen Thomas**, **William Jones**, **Luke Williams**, **Sarah Roberts**, **Ross Doherty**, **Lucy Pritchard**, **Mark Smith**, **Archie Lush**) all singing. They are also patients and staff from the ward.* **Mr Orchard** *is somehow monstrous.*

Part 1 – The Caning

Schoolkids   'I hear thy welcome voice, That calls me, Lord, to thee; For cleansing in thy precious blood, That flow'd on Calvary. I am coming, Lord! / Coming –'

Mr Orchard *sees* **Nye**.

Mr Orchard   Bevan! Where do you think you're going? Trying to escape. Stand up! Don't slouch. Straight, I said . . . Your sister Arianwen is a star pupil yet you seem to want to get out of every class.

Nye   Sssssssssssssorry . . . ssssssir

Mr Orchard   Seats.

The school children run to their seats.

Mr Orchard   Page one. Together.

Schoolkids   I wandered lonely as a cloud that floats on high o'er vales / and hills

Mr Orchard   Jones, Neil, take over. Loud and clear, enunciate every word, please.

Neil   When all at once I saw a crowd

Mr Orchard   Jones, William take over.

William   A host, of golden daffodils.

Mr Orchard   Pritchard!

Lucy   Beside the lake, beneath the trees

Mr Orchard   Bevan!

Nye   Fffffl . . . Fluttttttring and d-d-ddd dd.

Mr Orchard   Dancing!

Nye   Ddddd d ddd

Mr Orchard   Everyone is waiting, Bevan.

Beat.

Fluttering and dancing in the breeze. Next line.

Nye   C-c-ccc-c-ccc-ccc

Mr Orchard   ENUNCIATE! CONTINUOUS! Spit, it, out, boy! Continuous! Enunciate!

Nye   C-c-coontt -tttt-tt t–

Mr Orchard   Continuous! Don't look down! What are you looking at your shoes for?

Continuous as the stars that shine

Beat.

Don't shake your head at me. You will say continuous, or I will cane you.

Silence.

Nye   Cc cc . . .

Mr Orchard   Continuous.

Nye   Cc-ccc-ccc . . .

Mr Orchard   Continuous.

Nye   Tsssss.

Mr Orchard   CONTINUOUS CONTINUOUS /
CONTINUOUS!

Nye   I CAN'T!

Archie   He's gorra a stutter, sir, why don' you ask one of us to read?

Mr Orchard   Because, Lush, you all need to learn self-reliance! No-one is going to look after you when you leave school. Bevan, give me your hand. Hand, Bevan.

Nye   I-III . . .

Mr Orchard   HAND, BEVAN, NOW!

Silence.

Say continuous.

Nye   C-cccc

Mr Orchard *canes* **Nye***'s hand.*

Nye   AAAoooww!!

Mr Orchard   Continuous!

Nye   Ccc-ccc-c-ccc

Mr Orchard *canes* **Nye***'s hand.*

Nye   Awwwoooo.

Mr Orchard   Continuous.

Mr Orchard *prepares to swipe.*

Archie   Continuous.

Nye   Continuous.

Mr Orchard *has to stop himself.*

Mr Orchard   Lush! Stay out of this. Continuous as the stars that shine

Nye   As the sssssss-sss-ssss-ss

Archie   Stars!

Nye   Stars

Archie   That

Nye   That

Archie   Shine

Nye   Shine

Mr Orchard *has to drop his cane.*

Mr Orchard   One more word out of you, Lush, and I swear I will cane you too! Continuous as the stars that shine.

Nye   C-cc-cccc

Archie   Continuous.

Nye   Continuous . . .

Mr Orchard   Lush, step forward.

Nye   Nnno no nnnnno nnnooo. NNnnnnooo s ssssssssir he was just he was jus' 'elping ssssssssss. Ssssssss. Sssssss ir.

Mr Orchard   Hand.

Nye   NNNnnnnoo nnnnno nnnnnoo sssssssir ah he ah ssssssiii nnnnnnoo he was jus' he was 'elping . . .

Mr Orchard   Hand out, Lush.

Archie *puts his hand out.*

Mr Orchard *is about to swipe when* **Nye** *puts his hand on top of* **Archie***'s.*

A moment.

Mr Orchard   Move. Move your hand, Bevan, or you will get ten strokes for disobedience.

Nye *doesn't move.*

Nye   Nnnnooo, sir.

Mr Orchard   Fine. I will cane you until you move your hand.

Mr Orchard *raises his hand to swipe . . .*

And then **Lucy** *runs and puts her hand on* **Nye***'s.*

Mr Orchard   What are you doing?

And **Neil** *and* **Owen** *and* **Gwen***.*

Mr Orchard   What are you doing? Sit down!

Lucy   No / sir.

Neil   We're not sitting down, sir.

Owen   Nor / us, sir.

Gwen   Not fair, sir / and you know it.

William   We're not sitting down until you stop caning them, sir.

And **William***,* **Mark***,* **Ross***,* **Sarah***, everyone else except* **Luke** *has their hands on* **Archie***'s.*

Mr Orchard   SIT DOWN NOW! THE LOT OF YOU!

Mr Orchard *swipes his cane, the children pull their hands away.*

Part 2 – The Fightback

Nye *steps towards* **Mr Orchard**.

Nye   Not until you sssssstop ttt-t-trying to hit everyone.

Mr Orchard *swings his cane to strike* **Nye**, *the children rush* **Mr Orchard** *and bundle him.*

Neil   Stop it, sir! / You can't be trying to hit everyone.

Gwen   Get him! / Put him over there.

Owen   You can't / do this, sir.

Mr Orchard   WHAT THE HELL DO YOU THINK YOU'RE DOING! PUT ME DOWN IMMEDIATELY!

Mr Orchard *swipes for the children.*

Nye   Sir! You're out of c-c-c-c-control, sir!

Mr Orchard's *attention is drawn to* **Nye**; *he approaches him.*

Mr Orchard   I'll show you control! I have never heard so much insolence in all of my days.

Mr Orchard *goes to attack* **Nye** *again; the class swarm* **Mr Orchard** *again.*

Part 3 – The Bundle

Neil   Pin him down! Hold him down!

Ross   Hold him / down, Hold him down!

Sarah   Please, sir / we're trying to help!

Mark   Get his / cane off him!

Lucy   Grab his cane!

Mr Orchard *breaks free and points a cane at* **Lucy**.

Lucy   Stop / it, sir!

William   Leave her, sir.

Mr Orchard   In your / seat, Pritchard.

Lucy   No, sir!

Archie   You can't do this, / sir!

Nye   You're gonna g-g-g-get sssssacked, sir!

Mr Orchard   I will make sure that every single one of you is expelled.

Luke   I'd like it known that I have had nothing to do with this.

Neil   When I tell Mr Hopkins he's gonna sack you.

Mr Orchard *lunges for* **Neil**.

Mr Orchard   Don't threaten me, Jones!

Mr Orchard *lunges at the group*.

Part 4 – Orchard Fights Back

Archie   I'm telling!

Archie *exits*.

Nye   You need to calm down.

Mr Orchard *turns towards* **Nye**.

Mr Orchard   You, Bevan! You started this insurrection. I'll make sure Mr Hopkins holds you down / himself while I –

The children protect **Nye**.

The children behind **Mr Orchard** *grab him*.

Ross   Grab / him! Put him over there!

Sarah   You'll make it worse.

Neil   Put / him in the bin!

Gwen   You / have to stop, sir!

Owen   Grab / his cane!

Mr Orchard   Put me down! How dare you put your hands on me? / Put me down immediately.

Mark   If you want us to listen to you, you'd better start treating us with some respect!

Mr Orchard   Shut your mouth, Smith.

Mr Orchard *traps* **Mark**.

Part 5 – The Final Battle

Nye   You shut up, sir! You're a ffff-fucking mmhm a-bully! And everyone knows it!

Mark *escapes and* **Mr Orchard** *swipes towards* **Nye**.

Lucy   You're gonna get sacked, sir!

Mr Orchard *swipes for* **Lucy**.

Neil   What's he doing?

Gwen   He's gone mad!

Mr Orchard *swipes again*.

Mr Orchard   Shut your mouths!

William   PLEASE, SIR!

Neil   My dad said you were prick, sir!

Mr Orchard *lunges for* **Neil** *and strikes* **Luke** *by accident*.

The children circle **Mr Orchard**, *and* **Mr Orchard** *swipes for every one of them in every direction*.

Mr Orchard   ALL OF YOU WILL RECEIVE FIFTY CANES EACH.

Mr Orchard *is about to strike* **Ross**.

Ross   I ain't done nothing, sir!

Nye   I'm the one you want!

Mr Orchard *chases* **Nye** *around the chair, all the children run and hide.*

Nye *is left on his own . . .* **Mr Orchard** *towers over* **Nye** *with his cane.*

Sarah   Quick, / get Mr Hopkins!

William   Go / go go!

Mark   Run / run, get Mr Hopkins!!

Gwen   Stop blaming Nye!

Neil   You're just picking on him because you're a bully!

Mr Orchard   If you won't learn through instruction then you will learn through / pain.

Scene Four

NHS Royal Free Hospital Hampstead 1960

Archie   Here you are. I can't find the doctor anywhere.

Jennie   He's just been.

Archie   Oh, did I miss him?

Jennie   Nye was in a lot of pain so they sedated him.

Archie *looks to* **Nye**.

Archie   Is he?

Jennie   He's sleeping.

Archie   I wanted to be here. Bloody hell, I wanted to be here.

Beat.

Is he? Was he? How was he with the news?

Jennie   Oh. We didn't . . .

Archie   Oh? Oh OK.

Jennie   Wasn't really / . . . the time

Archie   OK. But, the doctor saw him, Doctor Dain saw him?

Jennie   Yes.

Archie   Didn't he say / anything or?

Jennie   He'd just woken up.

Archie   Right, of course.

Jennie   Wasn't the right time.

Archie   What did Dain say then?

Jennie   He just said. You know, he told Nye . . . everything went fine and that he'd speak to him later.

Archie   OK, and Nye didn't cotton on to anything?

Jennie   No.

Archie   When he wakes up next time, he'll be more rested, the pain will be under control, it makes more sense. He'll be able to absorb it.

Jennie   Yes. I suppose.

Archie   He will, he'll be fine.

Jennie   Yes, well, we'll see.

Archie   He will.

Beat.

Jennie   I just don't want to worry him unnecessarily.

Archie   He's gonna be worried. We're all gonna be worried.

Jennie   I know.

Beat.

That's why I thought maybe. Actually. It's best we don't tell him.

Archie   But. What about? Sorry. What?

Jennie   That way whatever time he has, he doesn't spend it worrying or sad or upset. Or scared.

Archie   He would want to know.

Jennie   Would he?

Archie   Yes.

Jennie   Would he though?

Archie   Yes. He would. Absolutely.

Jennie   I don't think so.

Archie   We have to tell him.

Jennie   Think what's best for him.

Archie   I am and he should know.

Jennie   What's best for him is that with the time he's got, his quality of life will be better if he doesn't know.

Archie   That was never the plan.

Jennie   Plans change.

Archie   Why?

Jennie   He woke up.

Archie   So?

Jennie   He woke up. And.

Archie   And what?

Jennie   He saw the ward.

Beat.

He saw the ward.

Beat.

And.

Beat.

He had. He had a twinkle in his eye. And I know what that means.

Archie   What's it mean?

Jennie   It means. You wouldn't understand. It means he's dreaming. He's planning. I don't want to take that away from him. That is who he is.

Beat.

So we're not going to tell him.

Archie   I don't think that's a good idea.

Jennie   Well, this is next of kin stuff, Archie.

Archie   Shouldn't we . . . find . . . consensus on this.

Jennie   This isn't a party conference.

Archie   Look, if you're scared / you know I'll be

Jennie   I'm not scared. I'm not scared.

Archie   But, if you arc. Y'know. I'll be there. I'll be there and it won't be as scary as you think it is. Sometimes, you make things bigger in your head than they actually are. Like this one time, there was this elderly old lady, who was being evicted and I promised her I'd sort it. I tried everything, but I couldn't fix it for her. I was so scared of telling her, but in the end she was fine. She said, 'that's ok, thank you for trying so hard.'

Jennie   You're saying this is like a housing dispute?

Archie   Forget about the elderly old woman, forget about her, that's not the point. The point is, this doesn't feel right.

Jennie   Well, I don't know what to say, that's your feelings.

Archie   You're making a mistake.

Jennie   I don't think you understand, it has been my main calling in life to protect him from things. It's been my purpose in life.

Beat.

If you'd told me in my twenties that I'd spend a large part of my life in domestic servitude to a bloody man, I would have laughed and then slapped you but it is just bloody typical that I end up with the one man who's been the best chance socialism has ever had in this country.

Beat.

It is some *deeply* cruel joke that my role on the road to socialism has been keeping the leader well fed and in clean underwear. I thought I was going to be Prime Minister. But we all make sacrifices for the greater good. And mine has been my career. So I have been his dinner party host, his wife, his lover, his maid, his confidante and principal advisor, the one person he relies on above all. I carry a lot for him.

Archie   And maybe this is too much for you.

Jennie   Fully participating in one's own life is a bourgeois luxury for most.

Beat.

This is just another one of those banal life details, that I will keep to myself so he can be happy for however long he's got. We'll be fine.

Beat.

You don't have to stay.

Archie   I know.

Jennie   That was a polite way of asking you to leave.

Archie   And that was a polite way of saying I'm not going anywhere.

Jennie   I'm done talking.

Archie Fine.

Jennie Fine.

Jennie *gets a book out, and starts turning some pages.*

Nye *sits up.*

Scene Five

Tredegar Workingman's Library 1908

Nye Where am I?

Archie Shh. Look at this. Look at this, this is my favourite place in all of Tredegar. I've never brought no-one else here and you can't bring no-one else 'ere, right. Promise?

Nye Promise.

Archie Shh. I'm serious, Nye! D'you promise?

Nye I promise, on my life.

Archie Swear on your mam and your dad's life.

Nye I ss-swear on my mam and d-dad's life I won' bring no-one else.

Archie Wha' you think 'en?

Nye It's nice.

Archie It's not nice, Nye, it's fucking / brilliant.

Nye It's ffffff-fucking brilliant.

Archie That's right, it is, it's fucking brilliant. Look at it, mun. My dad brought me 'ere once, and now I come an' read the comics an' stuff. And you can just sit 'ere and read wha'ever you wan', and no-one tells you you can't. It's called a library. You jus' 'ave to put the book back tidy like after.

Nye And we c-c-can jusssst. Read 'em? For free, like?

Archie   Yeah. The miners paid for them all. An' we can read 'em. We just got to put 'em back tidy like. An' then someone else can read it then after, that's how it works. And the best thing is. They get new ones every week. I've seen 'em bringing them in, in the boxes.

Nye   There must be thousands 'ere.

Archie   Yeah. Get one down. Choose one.

Nye   I carn.

Archie   Yeah, you can. Watch me.

Archie *takes a book out, flicks through it and puts it back.* **Nye** *is looking for an adult to unleash consequences.*

Nothing.

Nye   No-one's gonna say nothing?

Archie   No-one's gonna say nothing. Look.

Showing off, **Archie** *takes another book out looks at it and puts it back.*

Archie   Go on, give it a go, mun.

With tremendous apprehension **Nye** *finally chooses one. He takes a book off a shelf. He checks all around him to see if he's in trouble.*

Then being very careful, he opens the book and looks all around him again to see if he's in trouble.

Nothing.

Nye   I jus', I can jus' / read it?

Archie   Shh. Yeah. You can jus' read it.

Nye *turns the pages, reading.*

Archie   Is it good?

Nye   Yeah. No.

Beat.

Have I got to read it all, now like?

Archie   No, if you don' like it. You jus' put it back.

Nye *thinks about it. He puts it back.*

Nye   How many goes do you get?

Archie   You can have as many goes as you want. You can just keep trying them all. Get another one.

Nye   I can have another one?

Archie   Yeah. Sh. No-one says nothing. Look.

Archie *shows him. He gets two books out. Puts them back.*

Nye   So it's not like a shop. Or school.

Archie   No. And if you can't finish it, you can borrow it and take it 'ome and read it there and bring it back when you finished. For free.

Nye *takes one book down. Then another. Then another.*

Before long he has a stack he can barely manage.

Nye   I can't believe this, Arch, look at all these books for free!

Archie   I know!

Nye   I can't believe it. I'm gonna come here every day, and I'm gonna read this whole pile, and then when I've finished this pile, I'm gonna make another one and read that one and then / when I've finished that one . . .

Archie   You know. When it's just me and you. You don' stutter.

Long silence.

Nye   Dun really like tt-t-t-talking about it.

Archie   Sorry. It's just. Sometimes it totally goes. Like you don' 'ave one. So like. You *can talk*. You *can* do it. Why d'you think it is, though?

Nye   I dunno.

Archie   Why'd you think though?

Nye   I dunno, Arch! Fuck off, will you?

Archie   You fuck off. I'm only saying.

Nye   You fuck off. I said I don't want to talk about it and you're still going on about it.

Long silence.

Archie   You can tell me to fuck off alright. That comes out, no problem.

Nye   Well, it hasn't got a 'ssss' in it, has it?

Pause.

Anything with a sssss is a fucking nightmare.

Archie   It's mad how some words are fine and others aren't.

Nye   Well, welcome to my fucking life, Arch.

Beat.

I can . . . ssss-see them. C-c-ccc-coming. Like roadblocks in mmmy in my, in my sssss ssss-sen-tence . . . there's all these roadblocksss a-up. Ahead. I c-c-c-ccc-can sss sss sss-see them coming. I just can't a-get 'round them. And then I ww-wwww-worry about it, I think oh shit sssssss-see has a s at the ssss-start of it. I'm I'm a-gonna sssss-stutter on tha' and then, ww-when I get to it. It's even worse 'cause I've been www-worrying about it the whole time.

Silence.

Archie   Is that why you do that weird thing with your neck?

Nye   Sometimes I pull a muscle and I can't turn my head. And then I have to lie to my mam and tell her I've got a bad tummy so I don't have to go to school and I then, I just lie in bed not moving and not talking. It's a nightmare. That's when I think, you know . . .

Archie   Y'need help.

Nye   That I shouldn't exist.

Pause.

Archie   No. You just need to stop saying see.

Nye   How the fuck can I do that, / Arch?

Archie   I dunno. If you can see it coming just dodge it. / You know it's coming.

Nye   I fucking do but it's hard to think of another word to switch it with. That's how I get by most of the time. Tricks and switching words but it's hard to think of them.

Archie   Arianwen knows loads of words.

Nye   Yeah 'cause she's always got her head in a bloody book.

Slowly they look to each other – having the same thought.

Nye   Ssss-see if you can find another word for sssssssseee.

They run to the bookcases, pulling books out, flicking pages, swapping books.

Archie   Vis-u-a-lise? Vis-ualise. Visualise. You could say that instead of see?

Nye   Visualise. I can't visualise that happening. Visualise. Visualise.

Archie   I can visualise the words coming like.

Nye   I can visualise them coming. I can visualise them coming. I can sssss ssssss find another word for sssssss-say.

They pull books out, flick pages. Reach for more and pore over pages.

Nye   It's hard to find one. Enunciate? Enunciate. I can ssss-asay that. I can't sssssaasay sssssaay. But I can. Enunciate, enunciate. *Enunciate.*

Archie   You can enunciate.

Nye   I can visualise the words coming. And I can enunciate them.

Archie   What, what just happened?

Nye   I can visualise the words coming. And I can enunciate them.

Archie   You can talk.

Archie and **Nye** *grab each other and jump with excitement!*

Nye   I can talk.

Archie   You can bloody talk, Nye! You're not stuttering.

Nye   I can visualise and enunciate!

Archie   And you sound posh as well, like. Clever.

Nye   I can't wait to tttt. I can't wait to ttt . . . Oh . . . bloody hell.

Nye *grabs another book, he flicks pages.*

Nye   No. No. Hang on.

Beat.

Yeah. I can't wait to *inform* my dad I've been here.

More delight.

Archie   It's working.

Nye   And now I ccca –

He gets another book and flicks the pages.

I can now *articulate* my words. These books.

Archie   They can't hurt you now, butt.

Nye   If I can't say a word, I'll just come 'ere and find another one. I'll find a way around *every single roadblock*. I'll just come 'ere and I'll read 'em all. I'll read poetry. Philosophy. The classics. I'll learn about science! History. Economics. Politics. Marx. Engels. Dialectical materialism. Socialism. Class struggle! Ideological control! Freedom of association! Collective bargaining! Blacklisting!

Scene Six

Upstairs – Tredegar Workingman's Library 1921–29

The Query Club: **Archie Lush, Gwen Davies, Jack Stockton, Neil Jones** *and* **Nye**.

Jack *holds some paper in front of them all.*

Jack   Read this. We're all on it. They denied it but we've got proof – they're running a blacklist. We are never gonna get work in South Wales again.

Archie   Is that true?

Jack   Look who else is on it, they're all out of work. Nye, you got us into this mess, you gotta get us out of it. How long you been out of work, Arch?

Gwen   It's not Nye's fault, this is the Tredegar Iron and Coal Company.

Jack   How long?

Archie   Nine months.

Jack   How long's Dai been out?

Gwen   Fifteen months.

Jack   Neil?

Neil   Eight months, three weeks and two days.

Jack   How long have you been out?

Nye   Three years.

Jack   Three years your sister and her sewing has kept a roof over your head and food in your stomach. It's done. It's over.

Gwen   Alright, Jack.

Neil   Shall we start talking about this week's book?

Jack   Fuck the book. Fuck this reading club and fuck
Marxist syndicalism or whatever the fuck we're supposed
to be.

Gwen   Stop blaming Nye / for what happened.

Jack   Why? It's his fault!

Gwen   We all wanted better conditions. We all took issues to
the foremen ourselves.

Jack   And look where it's got us, out of a job and on a
fucking blacklist.

Nye   Look. It's hard.

Beat.

We need a wholesale bb-breakdown in industrial relations
before things can change.

Jack   It's too late.

Gwen   It does feel like we're sitting around reading books,
waiting for the revolution and the revolution's not
happening.

Neil   Speaking of revolutions, this week's book was *The
Civil War in France* / by Karl Marx, shall we talk about that?

Gwen   Oh, / Neil, knock it off.

Archie   For / fuck's sake, Neil.

Jack   Shut up, Neil, fucking / hell.

Nye   We need a collective action / before we can . . .

Gwen   The strike's not / gonna happen, Nye.

Nye   When the t- uh conditions / are right –

Jack   The strike's not gonna / happen!

Nye   No no no, not a strike. Not a strike. The working
classes will c-uh unite around an event.

Gwen   A strike?

Nye   An industrial confrontation.

Gwen   Like a strike.

Nye   An event that disrupts relations.

Gwen   A strike. Just say a strike. It's a strike.

Nye   OK, a strike.

Jack   The strike's not going / to happen!

Gwen   It's not gonna happen after this (blacklist). We need a plan.

Neil   You know who had a plan? The French / after the civil war.

Jack   Shut / up, Neil.

Archie   Oh / Neil.

Gwen   Neil! Nye. When my mother taught me how to sew. First, she explained it all, the different threads, the different materials, the different stitches. She explained it all. But I didn't learn how to sew until I *did* it. We need to stop reading all these books and try something new. /

Jack   You're all mad.

Gwen   How do people get power without confrontation? Without violence? How do the coal owners hold onto power?

Neil   Well, after the French / civil war.

Collective groan.

Archie   Alright, Neil, you read this week's book, well done, but we're actually trying to talk about stuff here.

Neil   This is the first one I've actually read. I finally bloody read a book and no-one wants to talk about it! Put tabs / on the good bits and everything.

Nye   Hang on, hang on, hang on. Gwen's right.

Gwen   I am? I am. / I am.

Nye   How does the Tredegar Iron and Coal Company hold onto power?

Jack   They own all seven pits and they won't let me work in any of them.

Archie   They've bought up all the land to stop other companies sinking pits.

Gwen   They own all the houses we rent.

Archie   Most of the shops too.

Nye   And what are the checks and balances on that power?

Pause.

Neil   Until we talk about this week's book I'm not joining in.

Gwen   The county council?

Nye   The county council. What else?

Archie   Chamber of Trade?

Nye   Chamber of Trade.

Gwen   Medical Aid?

Nye   Medical Aid Society. Working Men's Institute. Justices of the Peace. Hospitals' committee. The Tredegar Iron and Coal Company have a man on every board and committee, and they make sure none of those institutions challenge the company's interests but protect them. That's how they get away with all they're doing. Longer shifts, less rescue teams, blacklisting. So, if we can't take them on with a strike, maybe we take them on in the boardroom and get these institutions to protect *us* not *them*.

Jack   It's too late for us, mun!

Nye   If they've got a man on every committee then we need at least a man / on every

Gwen   Or woman.

Nye   Or woman on every committee.

Jack   What's the point if we can't get work? If I don't get a job soon my dad says I've gotta go to Australia, he can't keep me no more.

Beat.

Gwen   Did he say that?

Jack   I've got till the end of the month.

The group are devastated at this news.

Nye   Some of these committees are paid jobs.

Jack   They're not gonna accept workers on these committees.

Nye   They might?

Jack   We're miners, coal-loaders, timbermen. No-one's going to elect us.

Nye   Why not?

Jack   We haven't got any experience in running things, we're all workers. They're all managers. We don't actually know how to run anything. We got no right to be on the boards or councils. We won't know what we're doing. I'm sorry, Nye. It's not gonna work.

Long silence.

I'm sorry. I can't do this anymore.

Jack *starts to exit.*

Neil   OK, I'm just gonna say this and then I've said it. But there were a *lot* of committees in the Paris Commune.

Gwen   Oh my / God, Neil.

Jack   Fuck's / sake, Neil.

Archie   Change / the record, Neil.

Neil   No, hear me out. Hear me out. The whole place was run by committees. Loads of them. And they were all run by workers. No bosses or managers anywhere. And they ran Paris. Why can't we run Tredegar?

Nye   Neil's right!

Neil   I'm telling you, it's a good book.

Nye   Why can't we run Tredegar? Miners, timbermen, why can't we? Why can't we? Jack. Hear me out. We are going to read constitutions, / articles of association and when we know how every one of them works, we're going to get elected, because what's the one thing we've got that they haven't?

Beat.

Time. We've got time. We'll be more knowledgeable, better prepared and more capable than anyone else on these boards. And once we're on, we'll slow them down with pedantry, and scrutiny, and we'll keep getting working people elected, until *we* have the majority. And then.

Beat.

Then, we'll run this town.

Quiz Part 1

Clerk   Welcome to our new town councillors, councillors Bevan, Davies, Jones, Lush and Stockton, welcome to Tredegar Town Council! I'm the town clerk and, if you're not familiar with proceedings, Mr Williams will carry on in the post of chairman on grounds of seniority; as long as there's no objection, he'll go first . . .

Buzzer!

Nye *accidentally knocks a buzzer.*

Nye *is startled and looks to his team. And then his button. And then his team again.*

Clerk   Councillor Bevan? Everyone's waiting, Councillor Bevan.

Nye   No no. I'm just . . . trying to figure out how this all works . . .

Clerk   Let's move on, shall we?

Nye   No, no hang on. Um . . . So . . . you know . . . I suppose . . . what uh . . . well . . .

Clerk   Going to have to push you.

Buzzer.

Councillor Davies.

Gwen   How long has the principle of rotation been in operation?

Clerk   Well –

Gwen   And for how long has it been shelved?

Clerk   Um . . . well . . . this is not something we normally discuss. Do we need a formal motion? I don't really know.

Councillor Williams   We don't need a formal motion because we all agree with the principle of seniority.

Buzzer!

Nye   Who agrees that the election of the role of chairman is not the concern of councillors?

Clerk   Well, we all agree that . . .

Buzzer!

Gwen   I don't.

Buzzer!

Archie   Me neither.

Buzzer!

Jack   Nor me.

Buzzer!

Neil   Nor me.

Buzzer!

Nye   How long has the role of chairman been decided by the Tredegar Iron and Coal Company and not the councillors?

Buzzer!

Councillor Williams   Every member here has been elected by their wards, and to suggest otherwise is un . . .

Councillor Hopkins   Unparliamentary . . .

Councillor Williams   Uh, unparliamentary language.

Buzzer!

Nye   That's fine, we're not in Parliament. And which part of my question was a suggestion?

Buzzer!

Gwen   No part.

Buzzer!

Nye   Excellent, so as per the constitution of the council we will go through a nn-nomination and election p-process for the post of chairman.

Archie   I nominate Councillor Bevan.

Gwen   Seconded.

Buzzer!

Clerk   If we can stick to the agenda and submit nominations for the chairman role into *next week's* agenda / that would help us keep control of . . .

Nye   All those in favour of Mr Williams continuing as chair say 'aye'?

Councillor Hopkins   A/ye.

Councillor Williams   A/ye.

Councillor Morgan   Aye.

Nye   All those in favour of me taking the role of chair say 'aye'.

Nye/Archie/Gwen/Jack/Neil   Aye.

Nye   Motion carried, I will assume the role of chair for the rest of the term.

Councillor Williams   This is not on the agenda for today's meeting, it is vital that council meetings are conducted in a professional manner.

Councillor Morgan   Is this even in the constitution?

Jack   Article 14.3. On the selection and appointment of chairs.

Councillor Hopkins   In the middle of a meeting?

Archie   Article 33.5 – emergency submissions to an agenda.

Councillor Williams   Even so, you can't change chairs in the middle of a meeting.

Neil   Article 9 – assuming the role of chair.

Nye   It's all there, I recommend you read it!

Quiz Part 2

Clerk   Very well, chairman Bevan.

Nye   As chair, I propose we scrap today's agenda.

Councillor Hopkins   You can't do that, how can we consult anyone if we don't know what the agenda is?

Archie   Article 33.6 – resubmitting agendas.

Nye   I open the floor to councillors to raise any mm-matters of their concern. All those in favour say 'aye'.

Nye/Archie/Gwen/Jack/Neil   Aye.

Nye   Motion carried.

Buzzer!

Councillor Davies?

Gwen   Why have the Tredegar Guardians not lobbied for special measures for the valley?

Nye   Councillor Hopkins? This is your area of expertise as one of the Guardians.

Councillor Hopkins   Um. Uh . . . well . . . now then . . . The Tredegar Guardians have written to / the County council . . .

Nye   Maybe we need fresh blood on the Tredegar Guardians board? Do I have a volunteer councillor?

Archie *and* **Gwen** *raise hands.*

Gwen   Me!

Nye   Excellent, Councillor Davies, you can join Councillor Hopkins on the Tredegar Guardians' board.

Buzzer!

Nye   Councillor Stockton.

Jack   Why has the Medical Aid Society not provided relief from premiums for those suffering unemployment?

Buzzer!

Nye   Councillor Williams?

Councillor Williams   The board of the Medical Aid Society decided that it cannot offer relief for those suffering unemployment / whilst maintaining its commitment to

Jack   How many trustees made that decision?

Councillor Williams   The board.

Jack   The minutes say there were six in attendance, in the articles of association you need eight to be quorate.

Nye   Do I have a volunteer to join Councillor Williams as the council representative on the Medical Aid Society?

Archie *and* **Jack** *put their hands up.*

Jack   Me.

Nye   Excellent. Councillor Stockton will join the board of the Medical Aid Society.

Councillor Williams   This is infiltration! / This is – you are – this is some kind of political trojan horse!

Councillor Morgan   Infiltration by Marxists!

Buzzer!

Neil   Why has the Working Men's Institute not ringfenced a budget for the purchasing of books?

Councillor Hopkins   The Working Men's Institute has a limited budget . . .

Nye   Councillor Jones will be joining the Working Men's Institute board with special oversight of the library.

Buzzer.

Mrs Pritchard?

Quiz Part 3

Lucy Pritchard   Why do I have to go begging to the Tredegar Guardians, writing letters from my sick bed? How can I get better if I'm worried my children will be starving or in the workhouse just because I got sick?

Councillor Hopkins   She's not even a councillor, what is going on here?

Nye   It's our responsibility as councillors to take representations from the community, I invite anyone to the chamber to question our representatives.

Buzzer!

Mr Llywelyn?

Mr Llywelyn   Why can't there be more nurses on the ward?

Buzzer!

Nye   Mr Leslie?

Mr Leslie   Why are overnight stays so expensive?

Buzzer!

Nye   Mrs Jones?

Mrs Jones   Why have the Tredegar Guardians not rejected the Government's cuts to poor relief?

Buzzer!

Nye   Mr Fury?

Mr Fury   Why are there so many paths in the park?

Buzzer!

Nye   Mr Howells?

Mr Howells   Why are our rates going up?

Buzzer!

Nye   Mrs Lewis?

Mrs Lewis   Why can't we build another hospital for the women?

Buzzer!

Nye   Mr Francis?

Mr Francis   Why do the drains get blocked every time it rains?

Buzzer!

Nye   Mr Hill?

Mr Hill   Why can't we get buses to the top of the valley?

Buzzer!

Nye   Councillor Lush?

Archie   Why haven't I been picked for any committees?

Ensemble   Why? Why? Why? Why? Why? Why? Why? Why? / Why? Why? Why? Why?

Clerk   Enough! Enough! Councillor Bevan! You have now been elected *chairman* of the Justice of the Peace, the miners combined lodge, the Labour Party, the town guardians, the Medical Aid Society, the hospital trust and the Working Men's Institute, as well as *Member of Parliament for Ebbw Vale!*

The band strikes up! **Nye** *grabs the mic and sings 'Get Happy' with the cast.*

As the song finishes, the ensemble vanish.

Dr Dain (*God voice*)   **How is he?**

Matron (*God voice*)   **No signs of discomfort.**

Jennie (*God voice*)   **His breathing seems erratic.**

Dr Dain (*God voice*)   **That will stabilise, the morphine will do its work.**

Jennie (*God voice*)   **Thank you, doctor. Thank you.**

Scene Seven

Houses of Parliament 1929

The House of Commons.

Speaker   Thank you to the Honourable Member for Worcester for his supportive contributions. Next we have

the maiden speech from the Member for North Lanarkshire
. . .

Jennie   I must confess that this dying House is not exactly a
place of inspiration, and I look upon myself more as a chip
of the next Parliament, which has made a rather precipitate
arrival than as one really belonging to the present House.
And I say to Honourable Members opposite that there is
only one explanation for this Budget, and that explanation
is that, in the eyes of the Chancellor of the Exchequer, the
people of this country are made up in this way – the great
majority of them are fools, and the remaining minority
knaves. That is the only possible explanation of such a
Budget as has been put before us, and I can only describe it,
as a mixture of cant, corruption and incompetence.

Nye   Hear hear!

Neville Chamberlain   I thank the Honourable Member for
North Lanarkshire for her full-throated scrutiny of the
Budget. One of the functions of Government is to try to keep
the House, and the country, from getting into hot water –
and sometimes, it has to put cold in for the purpose. And so
the question of balancing the Budget is one which seems to
offer numerous illustrations of the old saying that 'a little
learning is a dangerous thing'.

Beat.

I have been astonished since I undertook my present office
by the extraordinary number of correspondents who write
to me with some infallible plan for solving all the problems
of the economy. These ideas. I notice that they generally
embody their ideas in a pamphlet or some such thing. When
I hand them out to my experienced staff, they are always
received with a weary sigh, because really, the only practical
solution is a significant reduction in unemployment benefits.

Nye   D-d-d-does the . . . Honourable Member know that
winter is approaching?

Neville Chamberlain   I thank the Right Honourable
Gentleman for his interjection, and I can assure him that I
am fully au fait with the concept of seasons.

Much convivial laughter.

Nye   Is he . . . Is he ff-familiar, with the nnn- concept, that
half my a-constituency are unemployed and a further three
million in the country are (out) without work?

Neville Chamberlain   I am afraid I cannot offer any hope
that the Government have discovered a plan by which they
can avoid or postpone the approach of *winter*.

Much widespread uproarious laughter.

You see, human nature being what it is, to show people that
they can be maintained by somebody else in idleness, at the
same standard of living as those who are doing an honest full
week's work, is something which might undermine and
weaken the fibre and character of the people. How many of
the workers are wastrels?

Winston Churchill   Hear / hear!

MPs   Hear hear! Hear hear! Hear hear!

Nye   You know, Mr Chamberlain, the worst thing I can ss
– observe about democracy, is that it has tolerated you for
four and a half years.

Winston Churchill   That's / downright offensive. I demand
the Honourable Gentleman withdraw!

Ad lib MPs' outrage.

Nye   I shan't withdraw a word!

Tory MPs   Withdraw! Withdraw! Withdraw! Withdraw!
Withdraw! Withdraw! Withdraw! Withdraw! Withdraw!
Withdraw!

Speaker   Order! I ask the Honourable Gentleman to return
to his bench and reflect on his shameful remarks.

Nye   The shame is on you [Speaker] for presiding over this! No, no, when the banks were in d-difficulties, loans were voted for their ss-salvation, and we bailed them out in a *matter of hours*. They put the *whole* resources of the State behind the shareholders and the rich when they get into difficulties, nationalising debt for the privileged. Christ drove the moneychangers out of the temple, but you inscribe the title deeds on the altar cloth.

Tory MPs   Shame. Shame. Shame.

Clement Attlee   For the record, this is not the Labour Party's view.

Speaker   I thank the Honourable / Member for Ebbw Vale . . .

Nye   I look around and I ssss – can see men raised by nannies! Sent away to board! Educated in Oxford and Cambridge! Cocooned in privilege from birth! Have any of *you* been means tested? Have you? Hands up who's been means tested. Who here has been means tested?

Not a single hand.

Nye *raises his own hand.*

Nye   I was uu-uuh I was without work for three years. Am I a wastrel? Am I? You want to cut my benefits. For people just like me? How can you uu-u – a – comprehend the devastation reducing m-benefits will have on people like me if you have *never lived on them yourself*?

Neville Chamberlain   The burden cannot fall entirely / on the State.

Nye   Neither can it fall ss(solely) – entirely on families, goddamit!

Clement Attlee   Nye.

Nye   A fluctuation in the price of coal means thousands of men are ss- laid off across South Wales. Nothing to do with the qu-quality of their work, or their a-a-ability to work, but entirely to do with the p-p- capricious nature of capital and financial markets. You worry about weakening the fibre of the character of the people by helping them. Without m-benefits, people cannot afford food and they cannot afford doctors and medicine when they are sick. I say the State weakens the fibre of, of society by *not* helping.

Winston Churchill *mutters to* **Neville Chamberlain** *and they both laugh.*

Nye   I don't want to threaten the noble lord. But if we were not in this place, I would wipe / that grin off your face.

Nye *scrambles over the benches.*

Ad lib outrage – MPs start to leave.

Speaker   ORDER! / ORDER!

Herbert Morrison   Nye!

Clement Attlee   Nye, get back here / at once, this is ridiculous!

Herbert Morrison   What the hell are you doing?

MPs   WITHDRAW! / WITHDRAW!

Nye   YOU AND YOUR FAMILY HAVE THRIVED ON THE PROCEEDS OF BANDITRY AND SLAVERY / FOR CENTURIES.

Speaker   The Honourable Gentleman will withdraw his remark!

Nye   You're a collection of political gangsters! You use the sacred emblems of patriotism to further the racket of protecting profits. You come here for the purpose of rescuing this country from the evils which afflict it, but *you* are the authors of our troubles!

Members leave.

Nye *realises he is now on his own.*

Scene Eight

House of Commons Stranger's Bar 1929

A convivial House of Commons bar.

Nye *sees a young* **Jennie** *on her own at the bar.*

Nye   We haven't met, but I wanted to say, I enjoyed your maiden speech, Jennie Lee.

Jennie   Thank you. Aneurin Bevan.

Nye   You know who I am?

Jennie   Everyone knows who you are. Charging around the place like a rutting stag.

Nye   C-can I buy you a drink?

Jennie   No. Thank you. I'm waiting for a friend.

Nye   Ww-would that be the Honourable Member f-for Leicester East?

Jennie   It was really nice to meet you.

Nye *is hurt.*

Is he going to try again?

No.

Is he?

No.

He'll just play it cool.

He's not cool.

Nye   What's a guy like Ff-frank Wise got that I haven't?

Jennie *is shocked and impressed by his provocation.*

Jennie   A decent suit.

Nye   What's wrong with this?

Jennie   You look like a cross between a Welsh nonconformist minister and an ambitious stockbroker.

Nye *looks at his suit and then to* **Jennie***. And then to his suit.*

Nye   My mam helped me choose this.

Jennie   Your mam needs to find a better tailor.

Nye   Lost all my confidence now.

Nye *sits down next to her.* **Jennie** *did not want this.*

Nye (*to bartender*)   Gin and tonic, please. Double.

Nye *looks to* **Jennie** *and points to the bartenders.*

Jennie   Fine. Gin and tonic.

Nye (*to bartender*)   Two gin and tonics, please. Doubles. Can I ask you a question? When you look around a room like this and you see all the men this place attracts, do you feel like an imposter?

Jennie   I think they're the imposters.

Nye   I know that, but how many women MPs are there? Four, five?

Jennie   There's five of us.

Nye   Because I ff-feel like an imposter and I'm a man.

Jennie   We're both imposters, that's why this place needs us.

Drinks clink.

Can I give you some advice?

Nye   Please.

Jennie   You're quite charming. You don't need to steamroller everyone all the time.

Pause.

Nye   I am quite charming, aren't I?

Jennie *nearly spits her drink out.*

Nye   What's your office like?

Jennie   Cold, damp and miles away.

Nye   Sounds like North Lanarkshire. Mine hasn't got a ww-window.

Jennie   Count yourself lucky, the draught through mine is horrendous.

Nye   If I could only find out who's in ch-a-charge of stamps and stationery I'd ww-write a letter.

Jennie   No-one knows, the whole place is a mystery.

Nye   Tomorrow I'm going to the tailors to put mmm (money) a pound down on a suit that could impress a pacifist Independent Labour Party Scot.

Jennie   Don't take your mother.

Nye   I won't. I'll take you instead.

Jennie   No chance.

Nye   I'm serious. (*Off* **Jennie**.) I'm serious. Come on. Help me choose a suit.

Jennie   I am not going suit shopping / with you.

Nye   Why not? What else are you doing? What are you doing tomorrow?

Jennie   Well I . . . uh / . . . I've made plans.

Nye   No you haven't, come into town with me. We'll make a day of it. Lunch. Gin and tonics, cartwheels in the park and some overpriced suits. How about it?

Jennie   I'm washing my hair.

Nye   No you're not.

Jennie   Yes I am.

Nye   Why are you ILPers so stubborn?

Jennie   Maybe because we have principles?

Nye   Join the Labour Party.

Jennie   I'm a socialist. Join the ILP.

Nye   I'm a m-pragmatist.

Jennie   That's just another word for collaborator. Anyway, it was nice meeting you, Aneurin Bevan.

Nye   Nye.

Jennie   It was nice meeting you, Nye.

Nye   You're going?

Jennie   Yes.

Nye   Frank stood you up?

Jennie   I don't ask you about your private life, don't ask me about mine.

Nye   I'm sorry.

Jennie   I know what gossip is like in this place.

Nye   I'm sorry.

Jennie   And I won't stand for it.

Nye   I'm sorry.

Jennie   Not from you, not from anyone.

Nye   Look, look, I'm lowering my antlers. I'm lowering my antlers. They are low, / down on the a-ground

Jennie   What are you doing?

Nye   in a mm-public / display of submission and humility.

Jennie   Get up.

Nye   I am ssss-sniffing around on the ground and the shame I feel is so powerful my antlers are now dd-drooping. Look at me. Pathetic. And subservient.

Jennie   Get up, Nye.

Nye   And now I'm dd a-delicately, quietly, trotting my hooves around the room, like a downy fawn, so as not to cause offence to the *ss-supremely* dominant Alpha, but also hoping to catch the Alpha's eye, to ask if I may be granted the honour of walking her home.

Jennie   You're an idiot.

Nye   Nevertheless, can I walk you home?

Beat.

Jennie   Come on then.

Nye   Having said that, we've done gin and tonics, I think it would be naïve not to do dinner.

Jennie   No.

Nye   And then cocktails.

Jennie   No.

Nye   And dance late into the night.

Jennie   No.

Nye   Carouse with each other into the small hours.

Jennie   No.

Nye   And realise we're not drunk but actually intoxicated with each other.

Jennie   No thank you.

Nye   And the only cure is to wrap our bodies around each other.

Jennie   Dear God.

Nye   Until there are no secrets between us.

Jennie   No chance.

Nye   And it'll be so good we'll simply have to get married.

Jennie   I am never getting married.

Scene Nine

NHS Royal Free Hospital Hampstead 1960

Jennie *enters with a vase of daffodils.*

Jennie   We don't have a normal marriage.

Archie   OK.

Jennie   We're not like everyone else.

Archie   OK.

Jennie   I've had affairs. He's had affairs.

Beat.

You know he has, Archie.

Archie   I uh . . .well . . .

Jennie   You don't have to cover for him. Really. I hope he's had a lovely time. I know I've tried to.

Archie   I don't know what to say.

Jennie   You don't have to say anything, it's fine. I'm sure he's put you in a number of uncomfortable situations having to cover for his dalliances. It's fine, Archie. I'm not angry.

Archie   I never approved of any of that stuff. And I told him.

Jennie   It's fine. We don't have a normal marriage.

Beat.

We don't share everything. We don't do those. Chats.
Politics, yes. The messy complicated affairs of the heart. No.
We have, and have always had, private lives. When we first
got together, we were seeing other people. And. We. Never
really stopped. We've never been ones for bourgeois
convention. I know Tredegar has a special place in
damnation for me, but Nye was a full-blooded participant, as
I'm sure you know.

Archie   Hmmm . . . Well. Y'know I . . . turned a blind eye
to . . . anything I . . . why . . . why are you telling me this?

Jennie   Because keeping things from each other has not
harmed our marriage. It strengthens it.

Beat.

We have been through some. Very. Hard. Times together.
And. We've got through them. So what if we don't share
everything. The things we've been through have bound us
together. We lost a baby. Nye had always wanted children, I
wasn't so sure at first. But he wanted a whole litter.

Beat.

But. I couldn't. We never spoke of it. And he was fine. He
understood when I couldn't try again.

Beat.

I couldn't give him a family. So I promised myself I would
give him everything else he needed. We never really talked
about it, but that was sort of the understanding we came to.
And you know. His career is our baby. We became almost
one mind. He used to say our love is a garden he planted
and I tended, and he's right. It's our secret place we retreat
to, to rest, and heal, and to be safe, I suppose. It's the only
place either of us have felt safe.

Beat.

Archie   He told me. About losing the baby.

Jennie   He told you? When?

Archie   At the time.

Jennie   What did he say?

Archie   Just that it had happened. And that you were sad. That you both were sad. I remember him crying quite a bit.

Jennie   He didn't cry in front of me.

Archie   Didn't want to upset you, I'm sure.

Jennie   I didn't think he wanted to talk about it. I didn't think – What did he say to you?

Archie   I can't remember.

Jennie   Was he angry, with me?

Archie   No.

Jennie   What did he say?

Archie   He just didn't understand. He said. He said it wasn't fair.

Jennie *looks to* **Nye**.

Jennie   Did he blame me? Archie?

Medical equipment beeps . . . bongs.

Archie   What's going on?

Archie *goes to a curtain.*

Archie   Nurse?

Jennie   What does this mean? What's happening?

Nurse Ellie *enters.*

She checks his vitals.

Archie   What's going on?

Nurse Ellie   I think his oxygen levels are low.

Nurse Ellie *checks* **Nye***'s pulse with her fob watch, and checks his dressing for blood.*

Nurse Elle *buzzes the buzzer three times.*

Nurse Ellie   He is struggling to breathe deeply, his blood pressure could be dropping. His heart rate has increased.

Jennie   Why's this happening?

Nurse Ellie   It could be from the operation.

She puts on the sphygmomanometer (a blood pressure pump) on **Nye***'s arm.*

Jennie   Is he going to be OK?

Nurse Ellie   We'll give him all the support he needs.

Doctor Frankel *enters.*

Dr Frankel   Hello, I'm Mr Frankel. Nurse, what were his observations?

Nurse *reads obs.*

Nurse Ellie   Observations were normal, Mr Frankel. Heart rate seventy. Blood pressure one twenty over eighty. Temperature thirty-seven.

Dr Frankel   Blood pressure dropped seventy-five systolic, fifty-five diastolic.

Nurse Ellie *notes these down.*

Dr Frankel *starts to examine* **Nye**.

Dr Frankel (*to outside*)   Porter? Urine output?

Nurse Ellie   Maintained.

Dr Frankel   Signs of bleeding?

Nurse Ellie   None noted.

Dr Frankel   Bring the oxygen cylinder, increase the rate of fluids.

Nurse Ellie *raises the fluid bag higher.*

Dr Frankel   And we're going to move Mr Bevan to the high dependency ward for further support.

Jennie   Is he going to be OK?

Nurse Ellie   He's very sick, but we'll give him all the help he needs.

Nurse Ellie *leaves.*

Jennie   Is he going to wake up? What if he never wakes up?

Sound design swells.

Scene Ten

House of Commons 1938–1942

Boom!

Neville Chamberlain *at the despatch box as dust falls and the building shakes.*

Neville Chamberlain   My good friends, for the second time in our history, a British Prime Minister has returned from Germany, bringing peace with honour. I believe it is peace for our time . . . Go home and get a nice quiet sleep.

BOOM! War sounds! The room shakes.

Nye   WHAT THE HELL ARE YOU WAITING FOR?

Tory MP One   Don't undermine the Government when we're at war!

Tory MP Two   Support our troops!

Tory MP Three   Show some loyalty to your country!

Tory MP Four   We're at war! You need to support our Government!

Neville Chamberlain   Um . . . Uh . . . steel production for the first quarter of the year has been increased to a figure of
. . .

Nye   WHAT THE HELL ARE YOU DOING? WE'RE AT WAR.

Tory MP Five   You can't criticise the Government during a war!

Nye   WE NEED TO D-DO SOMETHING!

Clement Attlee   Observe the truce. We have men fighting, no-one wants to hear the Government is failing.

Nye   This is Parliament! This is w-where their voices should be heard! How many thousands of lives have to be lost before you Tories can be moved? Is that what you're waiting for? A national tragedy?

Death *nears* . . .

Boom! War sounds, distorted.

Everyone hits the floor. Dust! People cough and are dazed.

Everyone looks to **Neville Chamberlain**.

Neville Chamberlain *gathers himself before* . . .

Neville Chamberlain   As I was saying, steel production has been increased . . .

BOOM! War sounds, distorted further.

Everyone staggers again.

Nye   Tonight, we have *empty* benches here. Is it necessary to have a ttt-terrible calamity before we get these bbb-benches filled and Honourable Members doing their job?

Clement Attlee   I'm sorry, I can't defend the Honourable /
Gentleman's position.

Nye   The job has to be done! It is a bad business, I tell you. We need leadership!

BIG BOOM! War sounds, mixed with hospital sounds.

This is the closest one yet, everyone is knocked over and dazed.

Nye   What the hell are you doing? This can't continue! We need leadership! What is your policy on leadership?

BOOM, BOOM. Beat. BOOM.

Winston Churchill *appears.*

Winston Churchill   You ask, what is our policy? I can say: it is to wage war, by sea, land and air, with all our might and with all the strength that God can give us; to wage war against a monstrous tyranny, never surpassed in the dark, lamentable catalogue of human crime. That is our policy. You ask, what is our aim? I can answer in one word: it is victory, victory at all costs, victory in spite of all terror, victory, however long and hard the road may be; for without victory, there is no survival.

BOOM! BOOM! BOOM!

Everyone has to hide. The room shakes. People fall over.

Nye   You're worse than Chamberlain! We're losing every battle! Men are dying because of *your* incompetence! Ww- we're going to lose the whole war if something isn't done about it. No-one dares say anything because everyone worships you like a god.

Clement Attlee   I beg to remind the Honourable Gentleman that in the national interest we need to support the Prime Minister, not / criticise him.

Nye   I propose the motion that says: This House, has no confidence in the general direction of the war.

Silence – gasps and shock.

Arianwen   Nye, stop!

Winston Churchill   This motion undermines the morale of British troops fighting for our liberty.

Nye   It's not speeches in Parliament that undermine their morale, it is what they are experiencing in battle.

Arianwen   Nye, stop!

Winston Churchill   Criticising the Government in the midst of a battle . . .

Nye   We're at war! We're always going to be in a battle somewhere.

Arianwen   Nye!

Winston Churchill   Criticising the Government in this House breaks the parliamentary truce . . .

Nye   Events are criticising the Government! Events.

Arianwen   Nye!

Nye   You win every debate and lose every battle.

Arianwen   Stop it!

Nye   You plan nothing and improvise everything.

Arianwen   Nye!

Nye   You are little more than a synthetic military glamour boy.

Arianwen   Nye!

Nye   And this country deserves more!

Scene Eleven

Family home 1925

Arianwen   Stop!

Nye   Stop what? What now?

Arianwen   All of this. / Just stop it.

Nye   I'm trying to help.

Arianwen   Mam and I have tried everything.

Nye   Bath salts, have we tried bath salts?

Arianwen   We've tried bath salts.

Nye   What about lemon juice / in water then?

Arianwen   We've *tried* lemon juice in water.

Nye   Mullein leaf / extract then?

Arianwen   Oh my God! We've tried everything. Everything.

Nye   Maybe we need another doctor then.

Arianwen   Nothing is going to work.

Nye   Have you *tried* another doctor?

Arianwen   Have you asked *Dad* if he wants another doctor?

Nye   Oh, he hasn't got a clue what's going on, he can't say anything / (*Off* **Arianwen***'s hard stare.*) I mean, I'm just saying, we shouldn't be asking him.

Arianwen   He can make it known what he wants. He can communicate.

Nye   But / when it comes

Arianwen   You just have to spend time with him. Learn what he's trying to say.

Nye   I'm trying to get us some more time.

Arianwen   We can't get him more time!

Nye   OK, well bloody make him / more comfortable!

Arianwen   We can't make him more comfortable!

Nye   Well, he's not fucking comfortable, Arianwen! He's not. / I'm not judging. But he's not. And someone needs to do it for him!

Arianwen   Well, the bucket's there if you want to give him a bed bath! Or if you want – to try and lift –

Nye   Don't be pathetic / Arianwen, honestly.

Arianwen   You're pathetic! You avoid any kind of care and then when I ask you to go and see him, all you can manage is to *look* at him like he's a specimen. I need you to *be* with him. Spend time with him, reassure him.

Beat.

Nye   I'm not going to just sit there when I can be reading / and trying to find out . . .

Arianwen   That's what nursing him is!

Nye   It's not! There's more important, / more useful things I can do.

Arianwen   There's nothing more / important!

Nye   I might find something that can help!

Arianwen   A cure? Don't worry everyone, Nye's worked out how to fix black lung.

Nye   Oh piss off, Arianwen / I'm not talking to you when you're like this . . .

Nye *goes to leave.*

Arianwen   No, no! Nye! / Stop! No. *No*

Nye   Let me / . . . out of the way . . .

Arianwen   No! You are not going anywhere. You're not. You're not. You are staying put. I'm not lying anymore! When he asked for you, I told him you were busy. I told him you *want* to sit with him. But you're very busy at the moment.

Beat.

I told him, sometimes there's even lawyers coming up from Cardiff to argue with you in tribunals. I told him you're out early and back late. That you sleep in the chair sometimes and sometimes you don't have time to eat.

Beat.

I lied for you. And I lie for Will. And sometimes even Blod. Myfi's here every day. But I cover for *everyone else*. He's worrying about us. He can't breathe and he's still worrying about everyone, so I cover. Because that's my job, isn't it? Protecting you, protecting him. Making sure *everyone* feels loved but never *accountable*.

Nye   OK. OK!

Arianwen   *Everyone* gets your time and attention except us. You see a gap in this town and you shove yourself into it without thinking about the gap in this family.

Nye   It's not that . . .

Arianwen   You've made me a tool to avoid this. You turn a blind eye to every / inconvenient truth.

Nye   I'm scared, OK?

Arianwen   I'm scared! But you exploit me. You are no better than every mine owner in this town, Aneurin Bevan.

Arianwen *leaves.*

With a mix of shame and courage **Nye** *pulls the curtains apart.*

Sound design swells.

David Bevan *lies on a bed fighting for every breath.*

Scene Twelve

Family home 1925

Nye (*to offstage*)   ARIANWEEEEN! HELP! HE'S –

David Bevan *gasps for breath.*

Nye   It's OK, Dad, it's OK Dad. Oh God oh God. PLEASE! ARIANWEN!

Not knowing what to do, **Nye** *tries to get up but* **David Bevan** *grips* **Nye** *in mortal terror.*

Nye   Dad, I think I need help. I think I need help.

He climbs in and holds his father.

David Bevan*'s arms flail and grip* **Nye** *in fear.*

The hands of **Death** *are the hands of his father.*

Nye   Oh OK. OK. It's OK. I'm not. I won't go. I won't go. I'm not going anywhere.

David Bevan *relaxes as much as he can, frightened.*

Nye *looks around . . . there's no help coming. He looks at his dad, who is terrified.*

Nye   They'll be back soon. Mam and Arianwen. Maybe Myfi will come with them too. Blod will come see you soon too. And Will. Will, will come round. And we'll all be together. Mam will cook something and we'll have to take turns around the table.

Beat.

Nye *looks around – no-one is coming.*

Terrified he might not live to see this, **David Bevan** *fights for breath again.*

Nye   No no no. Dad. Dad. Look. Just . . . Let's look . . .

They lock eyes. **David Bevan** *stops panicking and takes comfort from* **Nye***'s voice.*

Nye *watches him. He can't take much more. He makes the hardest decision of his life.*

Nye   Try. Try not to fight it, Dad. Don't fight anymore. Don't. Just . . . let's . . . look.

He strokes his father's face.

I'll look after you and don't you worry. I'm gonna look after everyone for you. I'm gonna look after everyone.

Nye *is totally alone with this suffering.*

His father dies in his arms.

Jennie (*God voice*)   **Will he wake up?**

Archie (*God voice*)   **I don't know, I'm worried he's in pain.**

Jennie (*God voice*)   **What if he never wakes up?**

Nye *startles – he looks up.*

Nye   Jennie? Where am I? What's happening to me?

Interval.

Scene Thirteen

Ty Trist mine 1907

Nye *stands in the dark . . .*

David Bevan *appears . . .*

Nye   Dad? Dad?

David Bevan   I want to show you something. Come this way.

Nye *follows* **David Bevan.**

Nye   Dad? Where are you taking me? It's so dark down here. I don't want to go down here.

David Bevan   This way.

Nye   It's so dark.

David Bevan   Follow me.

Nye   It's too dark.

David Bevan   Just . . . let's . . . look.

Father and son lock eyes.

Nye *is reassured.*

David Bevan   Hold my hand. Only in the dark can you see what your life is really about.

Nye   How much further?

David Bevan   Little bit further.

Nye   How much further?

David Bevan   Little bit further.

Nye   I'm scared.

David Bevan   Don't be scared.

Nye   How much further?

David Bevan   This is what I've been wanting to show you.

David *raises his miner's lamp and reveals an enormous, regal, seam of coal.*

David Bevan   Touch it.

Beat.

Go on, touch it.

Beat.

Nye   It's so cold.

Beat.

David Bevan   It's so pure.

Beat.

Give me your hand. See. Feel the seam. See. Feel the seam. Cuts the earth. Like a tree root. See how she moves? Full of power. Like a horse. You ever felt a horse's neck? The power. Feel it. Go on. Feel it. Come on! Feel it. How can you mine it, if you don't feel it? Now. See how she twists and turns? See? This is all we have to look at. So look. Other jobs. You can read the paper. Make a phone call. Look out the window, watch the world go by. All we've got is the seam. Show it respect. Tell the truth and the seam will give you everything. But if you get it wrong, you're scratching around on your hands and knees for days, wondering what you've done wrong. Now. Feel this. Go on. Feel it.

Beat.

Now, the bad miner just hacks away at this all day, and it's splitting and you have to climb up in there on your hands and knees. But the true miner, the learned miner, gets to know it. And finds the point where one true blow will bring it tumbling.

Beat.

Take your time.

Beat.

Study.

Beat.

Study what you're up against. Don't fear it. Don't flinch. Don't doubt yourself. Because one true blow can last a lifetime.

Nye *starts to follow the seam . . .*

He approaches the seam; he holds his lamp up to admire its beauty. He feels the seam this time, not minding the cold. He runs his hand along it and begins to understand better.

He runs his hands all along the seam, getting to know every part of it. He sees how delicate it is.

Scene Fourteen

Houses of Parliament tearooms 1941

Winston Churchill *approaches holding a cup and saucer.*

He offers **Nye** *a cup of tea.*

Winston Churchill   And here he is, the noisy member for
Ebbw Vale.

Nye   Prime Minister. Why are we . . . why are we in the
tearooms? You never come in the tearooms.

Winston Churchill   I visit the tearooms.

Nye   You never visit the tearooms.

Winston Churchill   I visit the tearooms. I like tea. Also, I
like to give them something to gossip about, seeing us
together. Biscuit?

Nye   No, thank you.

Winston Churchill   So. Aneurin. You have been my chief
critic throughout the war.

Nye   I have been your *only* critic / throughout the war.

Winston Churchill   And it has cost you dearly. Ostracised
by your parliamentary party, your constituency party is
furious. / You are entirely isolated.

Nye   My criticism has been entirely justified, I am perfectly
sure of that.

Winston Churchill   You are a merchant of discourtesy.

Nye   And you are a wholesaler of disaster.

Winston Churchill   Let's see if the rest of the country
agrees with what you have to say, shall we?

Winston Churchill *produces some newspapers from a tea trolley.*

Winston Churchill (*one paper*)   'Bevan the traitor.' (*Another
paper.*) 'Bevan the squalid nuisance.' I like that picture of
you. 'Traitor.' 'Traitor.' 'Treasonous Bevan strikes again.'
'Welsh windbag strikes again.'

Nye   You printed your own newspaper in the General
Strike, you might as well be doing the same now.

Winston Churchill   Whatever reputation you had before the war as a principled agitator, you've destroyed it. And now, you're the most hated man in Britain. Aren't you? Excrement in the mail. Death threats. You're assaulted in the street, the security services tell me, I know. You are *universally* despised. After Hitler, the next person the country hates / is you.

Nye   Everyone else is too scared. You have the whole House eating out of the palm of your hand.

Winston Churchill   We're at war.

Nye   I am protecting the principles of the House.

Winston Churchill   If I don't win, there is / *no House*.

Nye   I won't defeat one dictator by creating another!

Winston Churchill   I'm the best chance / we have of defeating Fascism.

Nye   A vote for you is a vote for the very conditions that have *led* to the rise of Fascism! You conscript men to mine coal underground, and then you allow the coal owners to *sell* that coal to our navy for a *profit*! A navy trying to defend the realm! This crisis is a privateering racket with your friends lining their pockets.

Winston Churchill   I am the only chance we have.

Nye   It's a privateering *racket*!

Winston Churchill   I am the only chance we have.

Nye   And I am the only chance the working people have. The Labour Party has never been able to unite the working class. We've spent decades trying to educate through speeches, libraries, colleges, all trying to raise the consciousness of our class, and we've *failed*. The working class has never been united in my lifetime. Until you came along.

Beat.

With your statesmanship and your cigars and your
(*impression*) '*our finest hour*'. You did it in a matter of weeks.

Beat.

Because the moment the ruling class is under threat, you
need a united working class. You *need* a united country to
defend your privilege. So, you declare a ceasefire on us. No
more blaming minorities, or benefits claimants, or the Irish
or the poor, or the workless, for the harm *your class* is
inflicting on us – no, it's all Blitz spirit and 'White Cliffs of
Dover' because now you're under seige as well! So, you use
all your tricks, all your apparatus, your newspapers and
your emergency powers, and you've united the working
class! At last. Thank you. You've done my job for me. Once
Hitler has been defeated, the next enemy *is you*.

Beat.

Biscuit.

Winston Churchill *hands him a biscuit.*

Winston Churchill   I asked you here because I have a
request. I've called for a vote of confidence in my leadership.
And I want your support.

Nye   You want *me* to vote for *you* in a vote of confidence?

Winston Churchill   Yes.

Nye   I'm an opposition backbencher.

Winston Churchill   Yes.

Nye   I broke the parliamentary truce.

Winston Churchill   Yes.

Nye   I literally tabled a motion of no confidence in your
leadership.

Winston Churchill   Yes, I remember.

Nye   I have no confidence / in you.

Winston Churchill   Still. I'd rather like your vote.

Nye   Oh? We're going to do this / are we?

Winston Churchill   We're going to / do this.

Nye   OK. You've lost Norway, Malaya, Crete, thousands of men have died, we've had ships sunk in the Pacific, you've lost more battles than you've won. You have no plan. You have no industrial strategy. I could go on. You're a great speaker, Wins – Prime Minister, but you are a *terrible* military leader.

Silence.

Winston Churchill   Fuck off.

Nye   You fuck off. I can't support someone who can't / – canvass opinion.

Winston Churchill   Can't what?

Nye   Can't canvass opinion. Or seek advice. Or evaluate. Or re-evaluate.

Winston Churchill   Like you, you mean? Have you ever compromised *your* position on anything, / ever?

Nye   I've certainly made / adjustments to . . . to my . . .

Winston Churchill   Here lies Aneurin Bevan who never learned anything because he was born with divine / intuition

Nye   I have / learned everything

Winston Churchill   Giving him sole right to be my chief critic throughout.

Nye   I have learned everything I need to learn about *you*.

Winston Churchill   You've learned nothing because you're a petulant child.

Nye   Well, this has been lovely; we should do it more often.

Winston Churchill   I can't defeat Hitler without American help.

Nye   Agreed.

Winston Churchill   I need to convince our American friends it is in their interests to defeat Fascism. That time is now.

Nye   Agreed.

Winston Churchill   Universal approval at home would make my dealings with our American friends more . . . presentable.

Nye   *I* make *you* look bad?

Winston Churchill   No. But you could make me look better. So, it falls on you to do your bit for the war effort, and vote for me. The stakes couldn't be higher.

Beat.

You seek power, but you're afraid of it. You demand to govern, yet insist on being ungovernable. You demand solidarity, but don't vote with your own whips. You are a born contrarian. The educated miner, the stuttering orator. The bed-hopping husband. The leader with no mandate. The brave coward. What you need to learn about power, Aneurin, is this: compromise *everything* to get it. Because once you have it, you no longer have to compromise. That is the privilege of power. Compromise. Vote for me. Leave the activist behind. Become a politician.

Nye *faces two doors, one with 'No', one with 'Aye'.*

He weighs up what he has to do.

Finally he heads to Aye, and steps through . . .

Scene Fifteen

10 Downing Street 1942–1945

A convivial ensemble meets him.

Civil Servant One   Good news about the Americans, Mr Bevan.

Civil Servant Two   Very good news, Mr Bevan!

Civil Servant Three   Not long now, Mr Bevan!

Civil Servant Four   Victory in Europe, Mr Bevan!

Civil Servant Five   Tide turning, Mr Bevan.

Civil Servant Six   Victory in Japan, Mr Bevan!

Civil Servant Seven   The troops are coming home, Mr Bevan!

Civil Servant Eight   Churchill defeated, Mr Bevan!

Civil Servant Nine   Landslide Labour victory, Mr Bevan!

Civil Servant Ten   We'll take that, Mr Bevan.

Civil Servant Eleven   Just this way, Mr Bevan.

Behind a desk sits **Clement Attlee**.

Clement Attlee   Ah Nye. Good to see you.

Nye   Clem?

Clement Attlee   Prime Minister, actually.

Nye *takes this in*.

Clement Attlee   I suppose you're wondering what you're doing here. Shall I put you out of your misery?

Nye   I uh . . .

Clement Attlee   I brought you here today to invite you to join the Cabinet. I'd like to offer you the job of Minister for Health and Housing.

Nye   Health?

Clement Attlee   And Housing. I thought it might be a good fit.

Silence.

Nye   This is some kind of joke.

Clement Attlee   No.

Nye   *You*, want *me*, in the Cabinet. I've never been a minister before, I've never even been a shadow minister.

Clement Attlee   Well, / I thought

Nye   I've never even chaired a select committee.

Clement Attlee   Maybe with some / support you could

Nye   You kicked me out of the party once! We don't really speak. Why would you possibly want me in your Cabinet, Clem?

Clement Attlee   Prime Minister. I sensed a maturing in your approach.

Long silence . . . is **Winston Churchill** *still there?*

Clement Attlee   Health and Housing.

Nye   What's your game?

Clement Attlee   There is no game.

Nye   Health and Housing?

Clement Attlee   It's a big brief.

Nye   You know I have a thing for Health, you know it.

Clement Attlee   Indeed.

Nye   And you are exploiting that, to what?

Clement Attlee   Nothing of the sort.

Nye   To . . . to to over-promote me? Is that it?

Beat.

So I, what? So I fail? Is that what you're doing? Making it so I expend my political capital with the left of the party. Is this a set-up?

Clement Attlee   Factional paranoia. I brought you in here / with the expressed

Nye   Addison's reputation was ruined when he couldn't deliver on Health and that was the end of him. This isn't a brief, it's a trap. You've got your feet under the desk at Number 10, with a massive majority, and you've calculated that the one person who could derail everything now is me.

Silence.

I'm the one who could split the party. You know, I can consolidate the left and hold you to ransom. So, you want to muzzle me with either failure or collective responsibility or both. You say factional paranoia, I say political chicanery, Clem.

Clement Attlee   Prime Minister.

The great disruptor and the great diplomat size each other up.

There's some merit to your analysis. Having you in Cabinet mitigates the risk of a split.

Nye   Thank you.

Clement Attlee   But. Have you considered that I may want to unite the party rather than merely avoid a split?

Nye   How?

Clement Attlee   By *delivering* for the left, rather than humiliating it.

Nye   . . .

Beat.

Nye   . . .

Clement Attlee   A united Labour Party, right and left in Cabinet together. Bevan and Bevin. Putting their names to the same policies. United. For the good of the party. The good of the country. The good of the people. The right aren't the enemy, Nye. They're just politicians you haven't worked with yet. And maybe you should try working with them.

Nye   As Minister for Health.

Clement Attlee   And Housing.

Nye   If I deliver you win. If I fail you win.

Clement Attlee   Welcome to Number 10.

He places a ministerial briefcase on the desk.

Nye   You think I can do this?

Clement Attlee   I don't think anyone else can.

Nye   That's not what I asked.

Beat.

I need to know; you think I can do this?

Another very long silence.

Clement Attlee   I think. What do I think?

Beat.

I think, if anyone can do this, it's you.

Clement Attlee *holds out the ministerial briefcase.*

Nye *stares at the ministerial briefcase. Eventually he reaches a hand out.*

He puts his hand on the case.

Nye   Thank you.

Attlee *keeps his hand on the briefcase.*

Nye   Prime Minister.

Clement Attlee *takes his hand on off the briefcase.*

He carries it in front of himself. He savours the moment holding his Holy Grail.

As **Nye** *lifts the briefcase his father's presence is felt.*

His father's love and pride is so present and so absent for **Nye** *that he can barely tolerate it. In this moment he is a minister for once, and a son once again.*

The ministerial briefcase twitches.

Nye*'s eyes are drawn to it.*

It moves again, violently.

Nye *opens the briefcase and is confronted with a sea of souls drowning in need.*

Patient One   Minister?

Nye   Yes, how can I help?

Patient One   You have to help, St Hilda's won't take my son because he's got polio and they only do acute medicine!

Nye   Your nearest council hospital will deal with infectious diseases.

Patient One   But he's got kidney failure as well, so St James' say he's got to go to St Hilda's, but St Hilda's say he's got to go to St James' – neither hospital will admit him! He's going to die!

Nye   But what if . . .

Patient Two   There's a diptheria outbreak in the schools, people are dying waiting to be tested.

Nye   Can't the doctors just prescribe the antitoxin without a positive test?

Patient Two   They're rationing the medicine! They won't prescribe it without a positive test! You have to help, my wife is being strangled to death by this disease.

Nye   Let me, let me see if I can get another centrifuge moved to your town to help with the

Patient Three   Help us, minister, my baby has TB, but they forgot to put the legs of her cot in tins of oil to stop the cockroaches climbing up. A cockroach got into my baby's cot, and now my baby's deaf.

Nye   Cockroaches? What hospital is this?

Patient Three   I don't trust them to look after my baby anymore but they won't let me take her to another hospital.

Nye   Give me the name of the doctor in charge of your baby's care.

Patient Four   Minister, my daughter has TB. And we've been waiting for a month to get admitted to St Mark's.

Nye   Wait!

Patient Four   She needs to get away from the dust, she needs fresh air.

Patient Five   Please Minister, I don't know who else to turn to, I broke my wrist, and the doctor can repair it but I can't afford the anaesthetic for the operation.

Nye   You can't have surgery without anaesthetic.

Patient Five   I have to work! But I can't because of the pain.

Patient Six   We need more ambulances in our town.

Nye   Which town?

Patient Seven   My husband broke his leg in the pit and he had to walk three miles home on it.

Nye   Which pit?

Patient Eight   They judge me, because of how I make a living. Don't I deserve care? Don't I deserve medicine?

Nye   Everyone deserves

Patient Eight   Where do people like me go when we're sick? I work on the streets and I'll die on the streets unless you do something about it.

Patient Nine   Please, Mr Aneurin Bevan.

Nye   Yes?

Patient Ten   They say you're a good man.

Nye   Good.

Patient Nine   They say you care.

Nye   I do.

Patient Ten   There's no beds in King Edward's.

Patient Nine   Minister, the maternity ward was overcrowded and there was a rubella outbreak. All the babies were born deaf or blind or with cataracts.

Patient Ten   So I had to put my eldest in the coal shed to keep here, away from the babies, because she's got measles.

Nye   If you can just

Arianwen (*God voice*)   **My father has black lung**

Nye   What?

Patient Eleven   You're the only person who can help.

Patient Twelve   Please help me.

Patient Eleven   There's no cancer specialist in my town so I have to travel five hours for an appointment.

Patient Eight   Please help me.

Patient Eleven   I can't afford the travel anymore, I don't know what to do. Please help me.

Arianwen (*God voice*)   **My father has black lung**

Nye   Who is that?

Patient Twelve   There are no ambulances so the doctor had to reset his leg on the kitchen table, the children had to hold him down.

Arianwen (*God voice*)   **My father has black lung**

Nye   Arianwen?

Patient Thirteen   I want justice. Or compensation. Or just someone to acknowledge that what happened to me wasn't right.

Jennie (*God voice*)   **Nye, can you hear me?**

Patient Fourteen   The consultant let six different medical students examine me and I started bleeding and lost the baby.

Jennie (*God voice*)   **There's something I need to tell you.**

Patient Fifteen   They won't take any responsibility!

Dr Dain (*God voice*)   **A duodenal ulcer.**

Patient Sixteen   Who is meant to help me?

Dr Dain (*God voice*)   **Six hours continuous.**

Patient Seventeen   Please, Minister. The almoner says I have to pay two shillings for my radium, but I don't have that money; if I don't pay she's going to stop my treatment.

Jennie (*God voice*)   **Please wake up.**

Patient Eighteen   My wife's mother can get penicillin in Newcastle but we can't get it here!

Arianwen   What are you so afraid of?

Patient Eighteen   Can you help get supplies to Worthing?

Patient Eight   Please?

Arianwen   Nye!

Patient Nineteen   I don't know who else to turn to.

Patient One   Please!

Patient Nineteen   Our GP looks after 18,000 patients. How are we meant to get an appointment?

Dr Dain (*God voice*)   **There were no complications.**

Patient Twenty   My two-year-old has scarlet fever. They don't have night nurses in the council hospital.

Dr Dain (*God Voice*)   **A fifth of a grain of morphine please.**

Patient Two   Help me!

Patient Twenty   She's being looked after by other sick children at night. What if she takes a turn for the worse?

Patient Twenty-One   Please help me

Patient Seven   Minister!

Patient Thirteen   I need help!

Patient Twenty   There's no-one there to look after her!

Patient Ten   Please help!

Jennie (*God voice*)   **Wake up Nye!**

Nye   HELP!

The hands of **Death** *engulf* **Nye**.

Scene Sixteen

NHS Royal Free Hampstead Hospital 1960

Nye *has a black oxygen mask on.*

Jennie   Nye.

Beat.

Nye, love. It's Jennie.

Beat.

Nyyeeee.

Beat.

Come on.

Beat.

Come on, love.

Beat.

Wake up.

She starts to shake **Nye***.*

Jennie   Nye. Come on, dear.

Beat.

You can do it.

Beat.

I've made a mistake.

Beat.

I need to tell you something now.

Beat.

I really want you to wake up now. Please. Come on, Nye. Please.

Archie *enters.*

Archie   What are you doing?

Jennie   Nothing.

Archie   What are you doing? He's sleeping.

Jennie   I just thought. You know. He should. He should wake up now.

Archie   Leave him be.

Jennie *tries.*

She returns to **Nye***.*

Jennie   Nye.

Archie   Leave him.

Jennie   Can you get the doctor, please?

Archie   What for?

Jennie   Just get the doctor.

Archie   Has he stopped breathing?

Archie *springs to* **Nye**'s *bedside.*

Jennie   Just get the bloody doctor, Archie.

Archie   What am I asking him to come for? He's fine.

Jennie   Get a doctor!

Archie   What for?

Jennie   Because I need to speak to him.

Archie   He's drugged up to / his eyeballs.

Jennie   Just do as you're told and don't question everything.

Archie   I'm not getting the doctor.

Jennie   Please.

Archie   No, I'm not.

Jennie   What is your problem?

Archie   I don't trust you! You're trying to wake him up against the doctors' and nurses' advice, you want to wake him up, but you don't want to tell him what's going on, you're just being selfish, / and I'm not having it.

Jennie   I'm not being selfish, / I want to speak to my husband.

Archie   You are! And I've had enough. This. Is madness. You're not putting him first, / you're putting yourself first. And it's not the first time.

Jennie   If I want to speak to him I'll bloody speak to him, it's none of your business.

Archie   No. No no, I've had to pick up the pieces of your meddling for years! Well this time I'm saying no. You're not doing it. You're not. You've done enough.

Jennie   What are you talking about?

Archie   You know exactly what I mean.

Jennie   I have no idea what you're talking about.

Archie   No, of course you don't.

Jennie   No, I don't.

Archie   I'm talking about you, dripping poison in his ear for years! You never forgave him.

Jennie   For what?

Archie   For being more successful than you, and every stupid self-sabotaging decision he's made, you're behind him, rubbing your hands with glee / at the carnage he's created for himself.

Jennie   Oh what absolute rubbish, you really are a pathetic / piece of work.

Archie   He burns bridges, and it's you handing him the matches. You have ruined his career. The more chaos he causes, with the party or with the Cabinet or Shadow Cabinet or with his family, the more isolated he gets, the more important you become. Because you want him all to yourself.

Jennie   You are a jealous excuse of a man.

Archie   Oh, here we go.

Jennie   You're not fit to polish Nye's shoes. You're nothing but a bloody leech sucking him dry for any ounce of status, clinging to his coattails. 'Nye's man in the valley', you're a bloody social climber, Archie.

Archie   Yeah, that's right yeah.

Jennie   Seeing your stupid nose in the air and your tail wagging every time there's a lord, or a president or some dignitary in the room. You're an embarrassment. Nye finds you embarrassing.

Archie   And Nye thinks you're a snob. Champagne with Nehru and oysters with Khrushchev. He'd bring you to the valley and we'd spend all our time co-ordinating you! Who you were going to speak to, who you were going to meet, who was least likely to notice your disdain and embarrass him. He was ashamed of you.

Jennie   He thought you were an intellectual pygmy.

Archie   He thought you were a political failure.

Jennie   He dreaded you and Ada visiting.

Archie   That's not true.

Jennie   It is.

Archie   It's not.

Jennie   It is.

Archie   I've always hated you.

Silence.

I used to think sometimes it would be so much easier if you just – He'd say, 'Jennie's having one of her dips, she's saying she doesn't want to be here anymore.' And I'd be sympathetic, and I'd worry about him and you. And then I'd reassure him it would pass. But part of me hoped it wouldn't. That you'd finally do it. And then we wouldn't have to deal with you anymore. And I think at times he felt the same. I think sometimes he wished you were –

Nurse Ellie *enters.*

Nurse Ellie   How's everybody doing?

Thundering silence.

It's not my ward, but I promised Mr Bevan I'd take care of him. Matron said it was fine. Is everything OK?

Jennie   Um . . .

Beat.

Could you. Could you ask him to leave? Please.

Archie   I'm not going anywhere.

Jennie   I'd like him to leave.

Archie   I'm not going anywhere.

Jennie   I want him to leave NOW!

Nurse Ellie   You know . . . this is a very hard thing for anyone to go through.

Beat.

Emotions run high. I'd encourage everyone to take a breath.

Beat.

You are the only ones here.

Beat.

And that can cause tremendous problems.

Beat.

But you *are* the only ones here.

Beat.

And that says something.

Long silence.

He looks very peaceful now. The morphine seems to be doing its trick. He's peaceful. Take some comfort from that.

Jennie   But he'll wake up again, won't he?

Nurse Ellie   I'm not sure.

Jennie   You must see this a lot, do people ever wake up? There's things I need to say to him.

Nurse Ellie   You have time to say them. That's what we can give you. More time with the people you love.

Scene Seventeen

House of Commons – Cabinet Office 1946

Herbert Morrison *appears.*

Herbert Morrison   Minister.

Nye   Herbert.

Herbert Morrison   Deputy Prime Minister, actually. I thought we could have a little chat before things get underway.

Nye   About what?

Herbert Morrison   Your health bill. To get it past the House, you have to get it past Cabinet and to get it past Cabinet, you have to get it past me. You've been very secretive. So before Cabinet arrive: tell me what your plan is.

Very long silence.

Nye   I'm not going to do that, Herbert.

Herbert Morrison   I really think you ought to.

Nye   Everyone needs to hear it at the same time, / otherwise it'll just be

Herbert Morrison   No, I think I need to hear it before everyone else. But no-one will share it with me, it's almost as if you don't trust me. You do trust me, Nye, don't you?

Nye   Well, everything's relative.

Herbert Morrison   Indeed. So here we are. In the Cabinet Office, waiting to build consensus.

Nye   . . .

Herbert Morrison   Come on, the noisy member for Ebbw Vale. I've never heard you so quiet.

Nye   If I run my bill past you, you'll make a counterproposal, and then they'll try and find a compromise between us.

Herbert Morrison   Yes.

Nye   And then you'll water down my vision. Fudge it.

Herbert Morrison   Your 'vision'.

Nye   Yes, my 'vision'.

Herbert Morrison   You mean your bill.

Nye   My vision.

Herbert Morrison   You've only been here a few months

Nye   I'm the Minister for Health and Housing.

Herbert Morrison   So everyone keeps telling me, but still, I find it hard to believe.

Nye   I'm a minister. Clem appointed me.

Herbert Morrison   When I think about it, it gives me two feelings at the same time. I feel excited slash alarmed. Two feelings at the same time, it's uncomfortable. So how about you put me out of my discomfort and share your vision with me? I'm giving you a chance. Do you want to get your nose bloody in here, with me now, or in front of everyone else?

Nye *looks around – he's on his own.*

Nye   OK. The health service is a complex mess, it is impossible to navigate and grossly unfair. The voluntary hospitals serve the rich, and the council hospitals serve the poor. The wealthy cities have all the facilities and all the specialists. And the poor regions are stuck with Victorian hospitals falling apart, so we're left with an uneven service across the country, where poverty is a disability and wealth is advantaged. In Sunderland, one GP has to cover eighteen hundred patients but in Chelsea, one doctor has two hundred patients. People are dying of preventable disease and illness, because they can't get seen, or they have to travel too far or the cost of treatment is too much.

Herbert Morrisson   So

Nye   So. Back home.

Beat.

In Tredegar.

Beat.

We have a Medical Aid Society. All the miners pay into it every week. And it covers the cost of six doctors and six nurses who take care of the whole town.

Herbert Morrison   There are friendly medical societies all over the country.

Nye   But this is what's different about ours. The Tredegar Medical Aid Society covers not only those who pay in to it, but also those who don't. Women, children, the elderly. In Tredegar, everyone gets the same healthcare as the working men. And it works.

Beat.

So, I want to. Well.

Beat.

I want to Tredegarise the whole country. A uniform service so it doesn't matter where you are, you can get the same service as everyone else; free at the point of need.

Herbert Morrison   That's your vision? Do what you did back home?

Nye   Exactly.

Herbert Morrison   So you want to take a model that works in a town with ten thousand people and apply it to a country of fifty million?

Nye   Well. It would mean nationalising the hospitals.

Pause.

Herbert Morrison   Go on.

Nye   Nationalise the hospitals. Doctors on a salary. Funded by central government.

Herbert Morrison   I see. It's very simple, isn't it?

Nye   Yes it is.

Herbert Morrison   Very simple. Yes, I suppose the challenge is the doctors won't agree to any changes when they can make a handsome living charging patients privately.

Nye   Yes.

Herbert Morrison   And then, the Labour-run councils take a great deal of pride in the hospitals they run and won't give them up without a fight.

Nye   No doubt.

Herbert Morrison   And on top of that, the voluntary hospitals won't give up their endowments and their prestige in teaching, and they'll be backed by the Tories because all Tories love to donate to the local voluntary hospitals to assuage their midnight guilt. So you're sort of picking three fights at once. Seems a lot.

Nye   Well, we need control of the voluntary hospitals because that's where all the consultants are.

Herbert Morrison   We could give them to the local councils to run? One less battle? Health service run by *local* government not central government.

Nye   But local taxation would mean the rich areas have the best hospitals and the best doctors and the poor have to make do. People are having surgery without anaesthetic because they can't afford it. No, a universal service needs to be funded by central government.

Herbert Morrison   But local government has a far more nuanced understanding of each area's healthcare needs.

Nye   What is our biggest obstacle?

Herbert Morrison   The doctors.

Nye   How do we get them on side?

Herbert Morrison   I don't know. No Health Minister has ever persuaded the British Medical Association to agree to anything. Their union is enormous.

Nye   Exactly. So we have to break their union.

Pause.

Herbert Morrison   Sorry. Did *you* just say that?

Nye   They're middle-class, it's fine.

Herbert Morrison   How are you going to break the union?

Nye   Pressure. And I only get pressure if I nationalise all the hospitals at the same time. Blitzkrieg. If there's a gradual approach, the Tories will unpick everything when they're next in power. It has to be a shock of change where we show the country what's possible. The only way this will last is if it's short, sharp and deep. A health service free at the point of use, based on clinical need, not ability to pay, is simple to understand and difficult to undermine. The execution of it won't be perfect, Herbert. But it'll be the closest we'll get.

Herbert Morrison   It's all a bit dramatic for my tastes.

Beat.

Thank you for sharing with me, but I'm afraid I'm not convinced. I'll be opposing in Cabinet.

Nye   What? Why?

Herbert Morrison   Because that's what a responsible
Labour government should do.

Nye   What does that mean?

Herbert Morrison   It means we're not going to undermine
our friends in local government.

Nye   Why not?

Herbert Morrison   Because we look after our own.

Nye   Why?

Herbert Morrison   You have the audacity to ask me, the
Deputy Prime Minister, why?

Nye   You're not actually Deputy Prime Minister, you're
Lord President of the Council, you just like to call yourself
Deputy Prime Minister. Why won't you work with me on
this?

Herbert Morrison   Because it's beneath me.

Cabinet Ministers slowly appear to witness this.

Nye   Why?

Herbert Morrison   Clem stuck you in here to shore up his
position and now I'm meant to take you seriously! You have
no ministerial aptitude. No talent for governance. It's
ridiculous! I'm here running committees, writing policy,
maintaining discipline, working every, damned, hour, God
sends, to make this thing *finally* electable and then when we
get in, we give *you* a seat at the table! And what's more, you
actually think you deserve it! Your sense of entitlement. You
swan around like some film star, dazzling the membership
with your wit and your charm and your stupid fucking hair,
shagging your way through conference, promising them the
world when you don't have the faintest idea of how to
deliver it! The thing about applying pressure is that you can
only apply what you can withstand yourself.

*He puts a pillow over **Nye**'s face.*

Herbert Morrison   They will do as I say because *I* am the Labour Party, *not* you.

Gasps from the surrounding Cabinet ministers.

Oh, uh . . . I didn't . . . we're all here, are we? Good. Yes. The Minister for Health and I were just . . . We were just discussing . . .

Nye   How Herbert's in charge and how he'd rather look after his friends in local government than the rest of the country.

Clement Attlee   I see.

Herbert Morrison   No, now that's not / how I'd frame things . . .

Clement Attlee   I think we've heard enough. All those in favour of Nye's bill raise your hands . . .

The Cabinet raise their hands.

Clement Attlee   Congratulations, Nye, it seems you now have Cabinet backing.

Beat.

Now. The doctors.

Beat.

The doctors have destroyed the careers of every single Health Minister for the past fifteen years. No-one has ever got close to defeating them.

Beat.

It is now your task to persuade the most conservative profession in the country to accept and operate this Labour government's most socialist program.

Beat.

Hit them for six!

Scene Eighteen

The BMA Negotiating Council 1946

Part 1 – The First Meeting

Nye   Hello.

Beat.

I'm. I'm the new Health Minister. Aneurin Mm a-Bevan. Who am I negotiating with?

Beat.

Doctor One   You are negotiating with the whole council.

Nye   Who is your leader?

Doctor One   We are spokesmen, not leaders.

Nye   Quite hard to negotiate with an organisation without a leader.

Beat.

Let's find some common ground. Where are our disagreements? Can you be specific?

Doctor One   One. No full-time salaried service for general practitioners.

Doctor Two   Two. Doctors will be free to practice without State interference.

Doctor Three   Three. Doctors will practice anywhere they choose.

Doctor Four   Four. The whole service will be based on voluntary hospitals

Doctor Five   Five. Adequate medical representation on all boards.

Nye   And which of those is your priority in this negotiation?

Doctor One (*at same time*)   One.

Doctor Two (*at same time*)   Two.

Doctor Three (*at same time*)   Three.

Doctor Four (*at same time*)   Four.

Doctor Five (*at same time*)   Five.

Nye   Who am I meant to listen to? You want different things.

Beat.

Is this why it's easier to just keep things as they are? So you don't have to find consensus? I don't think your members actually have as big an issue with my bill as you say.

Beat.

So, if it's not really the bill, what specifically are you opposed to?

Silence.

Doctors One/Two/Three/Four/Five   You.

Beat.

Nye   I see.

He takes a moment.

Then I should mm-make my position clear.

Beat.

On the points you raise. I will concede this.

Beat.

Absolutely nothing.

Part 2 – Labour Party

Herbert Morrison *reads a paper.*

Herbert Morrison   'Bevan has treated a not unworthy profession with the contemptuous derision of which he is a master.'

Nye   Yes / well . . .

Herbert Morrison   'Bevan attempted to bully the BMA and failed.'

Nye   It's not bullying, it's negotiating.

Clement Attlee   What am I going to do with you?

Nye   Nothing, just give me time, I have a plan.

Clement Attlee   That is the worst first innings we could have asked for.

Nye   I just need time, I need you to hold your nerve.

Clement Attlee   We can't have our landmark bill undermined by an entire profession.

Nye   I think I need to call for a special debate in Parliament.

Clement Attlee   What for? We've got the bill through. It's law.

Nye   I need to put pressure on them.

Clement Attlee   Another debate just gives Churchill even more chance to rile up the BMA.

Nye   Another debate gives me the chance to speak directly to the members, they'll read what I'm saying / in the press.

Clement Attlee   No, go back out there and find a way through.

Nye   But if we can just have the debate, my plan / will start to . . .

Clement Attlee   Your plan is persuade the doctors to change their mind or I'll get someone else to.

Part 3 – The BMA Negotiating Council

Nye *stands before the doctors.*

Nye   Maybe we got off on the wrong foot.

Beat.

Maybe, if we got to know each other a little better, things would be more collegiate. You, sir, what is your speciality?

Doctor Three   I am the President of the Royal College of Obstetricians and Gynaecologists. I am responsible for every pregnant woman in the country.

Nye   You're boasting. No? OK. I've read some of the things you've been saying in the press and the radio. I'm not the power-mad monster you think I am.

Beat.

If there is to be a National Health Service, then the power to administer it has to reside somewhere. Isn't it more transparent to know exactly who wields the authority?

Doctor One   You are answerable to no-one but yourself.

Nye   I'm answerable to Parliament.

Doctor Five   State control of medicine will destroy the doctors' clinical freedom.

Doctor Three   The State will come between the doctor and patient.

Doctor One   It jeopardises our Hippocratic Oath to serve and only serve our patient.

Nye   The doctor-patient relationship is sacred to you.

Doctor One   Yes.

Nye   It needs to be protected at all costs.

Doctor One   Yes. It is our responsibility to our patients.

Nye   There can be no interference in that relationship.

Doctor One   No.

Nye   Is it not an interference when a patient can't afford the doctor? When a patient can't afford the medicine? Or the surgery? When a family has to prioritise the health of the husband, and leaves the health of the wife and children to castor oil and whiskey?

Beat.

I consider the main interference to the integrity of doctor-patient relations to be personal profit.

Silence.

Doctor One   These negotiations are over.

Part 4 – Parliament

Tory MPs   Hear, hear! Hear, hear!

Speaker   I call to the floor for this special debate on the health bill. The Prime Minister.

Nye *looks around.*

Speaker   Prime Minister?

Nye   Clem? Clem?

Herbert Morrison   The Prime Minister is pre-disposed.

Ad-lib outrage and mockery from Tory MPs.

Nye   Uh. The uh uh a-doctors.

Beat.

They have dd-a-disagreed with every minister for health that has ever been appointed.

I am a Welshman. A socialist. And they find me even more impossible. So, if we can dd-dismiss that the dd-disagreements are because of my mh-personality, maybe we can look this challenge in the eye.

Beat.

We are not now dealing with the legitimate interests of the members of the medical profession. We are dealing with wholesale resistance to the implementation of an act of Parliament!

Ad-lib Tory MPs' outrage.

Nye   We desire to know if the Opposition supports that. Because if they do, I would warn them that the end of that road would be exceedingly unpleasant.

Winston Churchill   Is that a threat?

Nye   Do you support the sabotage of an act of Parliament?

Winston Churchill   We will not leave the doctors to fight alone.

Tory MPs   Hear hear! / Hear hear!

Nye   There is nothing noble about your support for the doctors, you have personally voted against the National Health Service twenty-one times.

Tory MPs   Hear hear!

Winston Churchill   You want doctors to be servants of the State.

Nye   I want doctors to be servants of the people.

Winston Churchill   This is the first step towards National Socialism.

Tory MPs   Hear hear! / Hear hear!

Nye   The nurses support the bill, are they Nazis?

Ad lib Tory MPs' outrage.

Winston Churchill   Hitler put the medial services under the control of one medical Fuhrer, this bill will establish you in that capacity.

Tory MPs   Hear hear! / Hear hear!

Nye   Now we've won the war, you want to tear us apart again.

Winston Churchill   Doctors of this country – do you support a National Health Service?

Part 5 – The BMA Negotiating Council

Doctor One   Following the debate in Parliament, we have held a vote. The results are in. The number of doctors in favour of the bill –

Doctor Two   4,734.

Doctor One   The number of doctors against the bill –

Doctor Four   40,814.

Doctor One   The doctors of this country will not be working for the National Health Service.

Part 6 – Labour Party/Press/Parliament/Home

Tory MPs   Resign! Resign! Resign!

Winston Churchill   Finished. The noisy member for Ebbw Vale is finished.

Tory MPs   Resign! Resign! Resign!

Herbert Morrison   'Mr Bevan's proposals were deadlocked, now they are dead.'

Tory MPs   Resign! Resign! Resign!

Clement Attlee   I'm sorry, Nye.

Tory MPs   Resign! Resign! Resign!

Nye   Where were you?

Tory MPs   Resign! Resign! Resign!

Morrison   'This failure must mark the end of Bevan's brief time in office.'

Clement Attlee   My staff will draft your resignation letter.

Nye *appears to be all but broken.*

Jennie (*God voice*)   **His breathing . . .**

Archie (*God voice*)   **It's really fast.**

Jennie (*God voice*)   **You must have seen this before?**

Archie (*God voice*)   **Is that normal?**

Nurse Ellie (*God voice*)   **It's what happens.**

Jennie (*God voice*)   **Do you think he knows I'm here?**

Nurse Ellie (*God voice*)   **He knows.**

Archie (*God voice*)   **He knows you'd never leave.**

David Bevan   One. True. Blow.

Nye *holds his briefcase aloft.*

Nye   I will launch my new National Health Service in three months' time on July the fifth, 1948, with or without the doctors.

He slams the briefcase on the floor.

It creates a mighty fracture – the one true blow causes a rumble that underscores the rest of the scene.

Winston Churchill   WH/AT?

Clement Atlee   No, no no no, don't say that in public, / you can't. Nye you don't . . .

Winston Churchill   You would / launch a National Health Service without a single doctor?

Clement Atlee   No, no, let's regroup and think this through.

Winston Churchill   You will create the greatest healthcare crisis in the history of this country.

Nye   I will launch my new National Health Service on July the fifth, with or without the doctors!

Doctor Five   If the health service goes ahead, every doctor will go on strike!

Winston Churchill   Doctors resist this authoritarianism for the sake of the country. Strike! For the very soul of the nation!

Nye *sees the doctors are cracking under the pressure.*

Nye   I will launch my new National Health Service in one month's time on July the fifth, with or without the doctors on July the fifth, but . . . Every negotiation needs compromise. So, in the interests of finding an agreement, I will grant the doctors the power to choose their *own* representatives on every health board /

Winston Churchill   What?!

Nye   The doctors will *choose* who they are answerable to.

Some doctors join the NHS.

Winston Churchill   You are trying to destroy the solidarity of the doctors' union with last minute desperate concessions.

Nye   Concessions, Winston, or compromises?

Doctor Five   The doctors will go on strike if the bill goes ahead.

Winston Churchill   Ha!

Nye   And if you sign up to my National Health Service, I will allow the consultants to work privately, outside of their NHS contracts.

More doctors join the NHS.

Winston Churchill   Civil servants! That's what they'll become!

Doctor One   The doctors will go on strike if the bill goes ahead.

Winston Churchill   Hold firm!

Nye   Also, I will compromise with the GPs. And I will allow them to buy and sell GP surgeries within the healthcare system.

More doctors join the NHS.

There is only one doctor left.

Winston Churchill   You shit. He has manipulated you from the start!

Nye   I will launch my new National Health Service in ten days' time on July the fifth, with or without the doctors. Finally, I understand becoming salaried workers is a concern. So I will make this commitment to you. I will make doctors the highest paid profession in this country.

The final doctor looks nervous.

Churchill   He's lying.

Nye   Join me and take the most civilised step any country has ever taken! And together we will build the greatest health service the world has ever seen.

The final doctor joins the NHS.

Doctor Five   The BMA negotiating committee recommends all doctors sign an NHS contract.

Nye   People of this country! We will build hospitals, bigger hospitals, with more beds so you can stay until you are recovered, so you return home ready for family life. Every hospital shall have their own specialists, with the right equipment, so you won't be sent around the country looking for what you need. Dentistry, glasses, mental health, all the things we need and to live with serenity, starting with universal healthcare for all.

Beat.

We shall never have all we need. Expectation will always exceed capacity . . . the service must always be changing, growing and improving; it must always appear inadequate. I don't want to give you relief. I don't want to help you survive. I don't want to give you medical care. I want to give you your dignity.

Scene Nineteen

NHS Royal Free Hampstead Hospital 1960

We're back in the real world.

The full hospital ward is re-created.

It is night time on the ward.

Nye *stirs.*

Dr Dain   Oh! Hello . . .

Nye   Doctor. How long have I been asleep?

Dr Dain   About fourteen hours. You needed it. How is the pain relief?

Nye   I could do with some more.

Dr Dain   I'll put you down for some more morphine. No other side-effects, anything of concern? Nausea? Itching? Hallucinations?

Nye   No. Well. Actually. Crazy dreams. Does that . . . does that sort of count?

Dr Dain   Mind if I check your stitches? Excuse the cold hands.

Dr Dain *examines* **Nye***'s stomach.* **Nye** *winces.*

Nye   Sort of, nothing made sense, but everything did. My life was all jumbled up. I was . . . I was running away from something. I remember feeling really anxious. Scared. And then. My father. Was there. He's been dead thirty years.

I was with him at the end.

Beat.

He died in my arms.

Beat.

Horrible death.

Dr Dain   Was he a miner?

Nye   Yes. Black lung.

Dr Dain   Painful way to go.

Nye   No dignity. And in this dream, my sister kept trying to get me to go and see him.

Dr Dain   Sounds like unfinished business . . .

Beat.

Nye   So, everything went fine? Thank God for that. I think I've been worrying that something went wrong. Thank you. Thank you, Doctor. You've been. Marvellous, really.

Beat.

(*Off* **Dr Dain**.) Is anything the matter?

Dr Dain   No. But. Something *is* bothering me.

Nye   It's fine.

Dr Dain   Is it?

Nye   It's fine.

Dr Dain   Well, let's see shall we?

He plunges his hand into **Nye***'s stomach.* **Nye** *screams.*

Sound design swells, we're still in the fantasia . . .

Dr Dain's *hand is in* **Nye**'s *stomach, up to his elbow.*

Dr Dain   Hold on! Calm down! Nearly, nearly got it. Hang on, hang on!

He pulls out his arm out.

What's this?

Nye *gasps in pain and shock.*

Nye   What the hell is that? It's a piece of coal. It's coal.

Dr Dain   Coal? Yes. It is.

Nye   What the hell is coal doing in there?

Dr Dain   How long were you underground?

Nye   Eight years.

Dr Dain   Could that be dust, coagulating? Let me see if there's more . . .

Nye   Wait, no, hang on!

But **Dr Dain** *plunges his hand into* **Nye**'s *stomach,* **Nye** *screams in pain as* **Dr Dain** *pulls out more coal.*

Nye   Oh God . . . STOP, please!

He holds a lump of coal.

Dr Dain   Something isn't right.

He plunges his hand into **Nye**'s *stomach again.*

Nye *screams.*

Nye   STOP IT! GET OFF ME! GET OFF!

Dr Dain *pulls out more coal.*

Nye   What does . . . I don't understand. What does this mean?

He picks up a lump of coal.

Dr Dain *fades away.*

Staring at the coal for meaning, **Nye** *holds it aloft for what seems like an age.*

Beat.

Nye   Surely . . .

Beat.

Why would . . .

Beat.

No . . . No no no.

Beat.

He takes some time to gather the courage.

I'm dying, aren't I?

Beat.

You opened me up and you could see I was dying.

Beat.

Why couldn't you, why couldn't you tell me?

Beat.

Why couldn't Jennie tell me?

Beat.

Jennie?

Sound design swells.

Scene Twenty

NHS Royal Free Hampstead Hospital 1960

Nye *watches on as* **Archie** *and* **Jennie** *say their goodbyes.*

Nurse Ellie   It's time.

Beat.

He's peaceful, he's not suffering. But he can hear you. Both of you. He's ready to hear what you have to say. It's hard enough. Don't do it alone, do it together.

Beat.

Jennie *walks over to* **Archie**.

Archie   I'm so sorry.

Jennie   It's alright, so am I.

They hold each other's hands.

Come on. Come on.

They go to **Nye**'s *side.*

Archie   Nye. It's Archie. I'm here. OK. And. I'll be here the whole time. And. Well. You've been a wonderful friend to me. And I hope you know, even though I never said it. I hope you know that I love you. I've always loved you, my friend.

He kisses **Nye**'s *hand deeply. Having said what he needs to say with dignity,* **Archie** *is able to move away.*

Archie   You talk to him.

Jennie   No.

Archie   Talk to him.

Jennie *sits close to* **Nye**. *She kisses him. But she can't. She can't.*

Archie   Nye.

Beat.

Jennie's here.

Beat.

She's got you safe. Like she always has. You haven't got to worry about a thing, because Jennie Lee's right by your side.

Jennie He's squeezing my hand! What does that mean? Nye, I'm here. Why is he squeezing so hard?

Archie Maybe he just wants to make sure you're here?

Jennie He knows it's me.

Archie Maybe he's letting you know he's here too.

Nye *nods, he feels seen.*

Jennie Nye. My boy.

Beat.

It's OK. It's OK. You can go.

Beat.

Don't you worry about me. I'll see you in the garden.

Nye *reaches and squeezes* **Jennie**'s *hand.*

Jennie *kisses his hand.*

And slowly **Nye** *loosens his grip.*

Nye Is this it? Has it happened?

The whole ensemble of NHS staff surround **Nye**. *He is caught and held by doctors, nurses, matrons, porters, consultants, therapists. The whole family of NHS carers carry him safely, with loving care and dignity.*

They carry him through a movement, a care dance, gently towards death. As he moves:

Nye I don't think it's happened yet. I can still feel. I feel scared but I feel safe. I can feel, people. People are nearby. I still feel. I still feel held.

The NHS staff carry **Nye** *and place him next to* **David Bevan**, *who steps forward with a miner's lamp.*

Beat.

Nye I'm ready. I'm not scared.

David Bevan   Hold my hand.

Beat.

Nye   Dad. Did I . . .

Nye *looks at* **Jennie** *and* **Archie**.

Nye   Did I look after everyone?

David Bevan *raises his lamp. The light slowly fills the room.*

Sound design swells with the passing of time. Now we hear things clearly: babies crying, monitors, heart beats, 'This will hurt a little,' 'Thank you, Doctor,' 'Nurse!' 'Count back from a hundred,' 'Feeling better?' 'How long has she got?' 'Is he in pain?' All the sounds of things that have kept us alive and safe and well and cared for.

A moment as the house lights come up and **Nye** *sees us all.*

A smile breaks out across his face.

Death *approaches with no dread.*

Darkness.

If screens are used, the following facts can be screened:

Within ten years of the NHS being launched infant mortality fell by 50%.

Death by infectious disease fell by 80%, resulting in a dramatic rise in life expectancy.

Every year the NHS makes over 590 million contacts with patients as it carries out Bevan's vision of providing universal healthcare from the cradle to the grave.

The End.

Printed in the USA
CPSIA information can be obtained
at www.ICGtesting.com
LVHW021531140624
783255LV00002B/291